Also by BRETT RUTHERFORD

POETRY
Songs of the I and Thou (1968)
City Limits (1970)
The Pumpkined Heart: Pennsylvania Poems (1973, 2011)
Thunderpuss: In Memoriam (1987)
Prometheus on Fifth Avenue (1987)
At Lovecraft's Grave (1988)
In Chill November (1990)
Poems from Providence (1991, 2011)
Twilight of the Dictators (with Pieter Vanderbeck) (1992, 2009)
Knecht Ruprecht, or the Bad Boy's Christmas (1992)
The Gods As They Are, On Their Planets (2005)
Things Seen in Graveyards (2007)
Doctor Jones and Other Terrors (2008)
Whippoorwill Road: The Supernatural Poems (1985, 1998, 2005, 2008)
An Expectation of Presences (2011)

PLAYS
*Night Gaunts: An Entertainment Based on the Life and Work
of H.P. Lovecraft* (1993, 2005)

NOVELS
Piper (with John Robertson) (1985)
The Lost Children (1988)

AS EDITOR/PUBLISHER
May Eve: A Festival of Supernatural Poems (1975)
*Last Flowers: The Romance Poems of Edgar Allan Poe
and Sarah Helen Whitman* (1987, 2003, 2008)
M.G. Lewis's *Tales of Wonder*. Annotated edition. 2010
A.T. Fitzroy. *Despised and Rejected*. Annotated edition. 2010.
Death and the Downs: The Poetry of Charles Hamilton Sorley.
Annotated edition. 2010.

ANNIVERSARIUS:
THE BOOK OF AUTUMN

A POEM CYCLE BY
BRETT RUTHERFORD

THE POET'S PRESS
Providence, RI

Poems in this book have appeared in *The Newport Review,*
Crypt of Cthulhu, Stone Soup (Boston),
The Moorish Science Monitor,
and in the collections *The Pumpkined Heart,*
Whippoorwill Road, Poems from Providence,
In Chill November, Twilight of the Dictators, and
The Gods As They Are, On Their Planets.
"Entre las Hojas" and all the poems in "Ring 2"
are new in this edition,
and the following poems have been revised:
"The Linden Tree in Prague," "Dead Leaves
the Emblems Truest," and "Not Years Enough."

Paperback Edition: ISBN 0-922558-59-0
This is the 194th publication of
THE POET'S PRESS
279-½ Thayer Street / Providence RI 02906
www.poetspress.org

This is book is also published in Adobe Acrobat PDF format
and in other ebook formats.

TABLE OF CONTENTS

RING 1

RING 2

RING 1

BETWEEN THE PAGES

All that I am is here,
even if what I am
eludes you.
I am pressed here
between these pages —
petals and stamen,
dust and pollen,
veined leaf
What scent
upon the yellowed page?
Try sandalwood and pine,
patchouli and mummy powder,
singed moth,
shadow of raptor wing,
a raven's passing,
a flit of bat,
a memory of lilacs.
You read my lines,
inhale me,
repeating my words,
my broken thoughts.
I am on your lips,
I fill the air
with green tea tension,
spark from your hair
to the nearest conductor,
then up and out the window.
Sing me to sparrows!
Teach the ravens
my autumn madness!
Recite to owls
my midnight charms!

<3>

ENTRE LAS HOJAS

Todo que soy
   está aquí
aunque lo que sea
   te eluda.

Me aprieto aquí,
   entre estas páginas —
      petalo y estambre,
      polvo y polen,
      hoja venosa.

¿Cuál es aquel aroma
en la hoja amarillada?
Supones sándalo y pino,
   patchouli y polvo de momia,
   polilla chamuscada,
   la sombra de ala de un águila,
   el paso de cuervo,
   los muerciélagos volantes,
   una memoria de lilaces.

Lees mis lineas.
Me inhalas,
   repitiendo mis palabras,
   repitiendo mis ideas rotas.

Sobre tus labios, nazco.
Yo lleno el aire
   con la tensión de té verde.
Me salto, una chispa, de tus cabellos
   al conductor más cercano.
Entonces yo vuelo ascendente,
   y parto por la ventana.

<4>

Cántame el poema
    a los gorriones!
Enséñales a los cuervos
    mi locura otoñala!
Recítales a los búhos
    mis encantos nocturnales!

<5>

AUTUMN ELEGY

The snow has come. The swirling flakes self-immolate
on hot maple grove, white-fringe the aging auburn oaks,
a coin drop from winter into the glacial lake.
(Cold comes so early here — September frost invades
the harvesting and gives the roses heart attacks.)
The boreal wind has taken up residence,
has seized the calendar in icy clench. The hat
I haven't seen since spring comes down —I undertake
a day-long search for hibernating gloves and boots.
My scarf has stolen off — I know not where. The mouse,
the gray one my cat keeps catching and letting go,
darts to and fro on the kitchen floor — does he know
the hard light's reckoning? Does bone-deep chill at dawn
embolden him this once for daylight foraging?
(We have an arrangement on the winter's supplies:
he comes out at night and he and I know full well
that whatever is not locked is not wanted, fair game
for a gray mouse.) He nudges a cast-off crust,
noses for crumbs, his whiskers italicizing
the advent of hunger, his tail a question mark
interrogating me about the wayward sun.
Alone in frost, I take my place at the lake,
my solitude complete, my steps the first to break
the pathway to the pebbled shore. I stand alone,
until the rabbit peers out from the graveyard grass —
twice now he's been there among the mummied lilies,
his eye, as mine, upon the never placid waves.
The summer boats are gone. White ducks that waded here
are huddled now beneath the bridge, far downstream.
The other birds have packed their bags — they have left us
their broken shells, their desolated nests, their songs
a carbon copy of a twice-repeated tale.
Lord Lepus, what do you know of impending ice?

<6>

Do you suspect the cirrus-borne snow's arrival?
Will you find greens enough beneath the snow bank?
We turn our mutual ways — you to your warren
amid the husks and roots and toppled gravestones —
I must go to book and breakfast. I leave the trees,
fond frame of my eye's delight, putting behind me
the cup of lake that always welcomes each sunrise.
Soon now its eye will be blinded, a cataract
reflecting sheet-white nothingness. I walk through town,
across the college grounds where last night's wind's caprice
made here a pristine bed of snow — yet over there
an untouched riot of maple on still-green lawn.
The carillon tolls the beginning of the day;
the students hurry, dumbfounded at virgin snow.
I am the only one to linger here. I stand
upon a carpet of red, soft, ancient leaves: some,
some are green yet, they are still proud,
they are fallen on the wings of their youth
and they are going to pick up anytime now
and fly back —
I am mourning for them,
for them, for you, for my brothers who have
fallen.

— *October 31, 1968, Edinboro, Pennsylvania,*
revised 1995, 1996

<7>

THE LINDEN TREE IN PRAGUE

for Jan Palach, Czech martyr,
who set himself on fire January 16, 1969
to protest the occupation of his country

1
Linden in Prague's Museum Square:
I was born, I was sown
of mother and father trees in some forest.
I screamed as the sun troped me out of the earth,
grew slowly in the shadows of tall buildings.
thrust out my blossoms at the hope of spring.
Years passed; I grew protective rings
around me. Exhorted into summer by sun
and the bacchanal of squirrels, I owe each year
millions of leaf-deaths and resurrections.
The solemn students and professors
stride by with dour looks, eyes locked
into the mysteries of Engels and Marx.

I must pretend to stand up straight.
I must not follow the mocking sun
    and its false revolutions.
I must wait for the ultimate paradise,
world's daylight redistributed for all.
I tremble as angry gardeners trim
the arrogant beard-branchlets
that fringe my still-adolescent trunk.
I am all passion and impracticality.
My heart-shaped leaves are on my sleeves
as I greedily drink sunlight, give shade
to those below in blossom-fall, exude the scent
that maddens lovers to *Unter der Linde* mania,
then paint myself in hues of gold and brown,
shedding my currency in one great shrug

<8>

as summer ebbs to frost-dawn.
Behaving well, it seems,
is not in my nature, despite those lectures
on dialectics I hear each afternoon
from the open lecture hall's window.

Much passes beneath my shadow:
across the square, crowds press
to bourgeois marriages and funerals —
the upright grooms go in,
the silver-handled caskets come out,
the church, the state, the people
move on in soot and sorrow, day to day.
On one side, Marx and Engels;
on the other, tradition, and just beyond
my line of sight that monument to Huss,
the great religious martyr. Conflict
divides us like the great Moldau.

We have lived through Kings and Empires,
bad governments and good. Everyone seemed
to think it was getting better last year.
But something has changed now:
Why do these people whisper always?
Why do so many avert their eyes from me?
Why does neighbor spy on his neighbor,
reporting every oddity to the men in black?
Why do I hear the rumble of thunder?
Why does the symphony break off
in the middle of rehearsing Smetana?
Why have the women gone to the cellars?
The earth shakes. Soldiers and tanks everywhere!
The streets are full of Russians and Poles,
Hungarians, Bulgarians, East Germans —
all of East Europe has come to crush us!
Men with fur hats speak swollen, Slavic words.

<9>

Death is here. The smell of blood is here.
My roots touch the entrails of the hastily buried.
Anger is everywhere. I hold my leaves,
make camouflage for lovers, conspirators.

Students rip down the street signs
and hide them in my upper boughs —
    the invaders drive in circles
    and cannot find their destinations.
I open my bark for secret messages,
encourage pigeons to carry the word
of where is safe, and who is betrayed.
I guess I am guilty of anti-people
tendencies — who would have thought?

<10>

Here comes that student, Jan Palach,
he's all of twenty-one, dark-haired,
a delicate face meant for poetry,
though worn by the study
of too much philosophy, too young.
He is the ardent one, the solitary dreamer.
And more: he intends to *do something*.
He and some others have made a vow,
a terrible pact. He will go first.
He is not Jan Huss,
      burned by his fellow citizens
            over the flavor of God:
he is just Jan Palach from Všetaty,
and he will burn in the world's eyes
because of Philosophy
      (Plato's tanks crushed
            the Age of Reason).

I am his unindicted ally.
The winter ground is covered still
with the dried leaves of my autumn,
some damp, some dry and worn
      to little more than vein lines.
He scoops them up; he stuffs his coat with them,
fills his cap, book bag and pockets,
fuel and kindling for his mission.
He is the icon of our unhappiness:
he will open like a triptych of gold
into a flame to embarrass the sun.
He opens the can of gasoline,
and before anyone can stop him,
he explodes into a fireball,
a flaring marionette; he whirls three times
then falls into a curled ball
of incendiary horror.

<11>

2

Earth gives him no resting place.
    As mourners gather
in ominous groupings,
the men in black dig Palach up,
cremate his already-half-cremated frame
and send the urn off to his mother.
There, in Všetaty, no one is allowed
to give him another burial.
No graveyard dares take the ashes
    for half a decade.
In Prague, Palach's first grave
is repossessed. The state deposits there
the corpse of a nameless old woman.
On your way now, nothing to see —
just some old cleaning lady's grave.
No Martyrs in this cemetery —
I'll see your papers please.

3

Twenty years on, a crowd will gather
for something called "Jan Palach Week,"
a pretext to take to the streets again,
and one day later,
    the Communist government falls.

Your ashes, Jan Palach, will return in Prague.
I will be beyond returning, for long ago
an angry axe man removed all trees,
to the despair of poets and squirrels,
the better to conduct surveillance
of all the law-abiding citizens.

<12>

There, on the spot of his immolation,
a bronze marker, half cross,
    both Catholic and Slav,
lifts out of mosaic'd pavement.
My last root is hidden beneath it,
as leaf by dry leaf, and ash by ash,
my ghost is a receptacle for tears, and memory.
I was there, around and within him.
I, too, exploded for Liberty.

*— October 1969, New York, revised 1986,
rewritten 1996; rewritten 2011*

<13>

THE PUMPKINED HEART

Somewhere, the moon is red and cornstalks lean
with the wind in plucked fields. Not in New York,
city of bleached stone and desperate trees,
is my long walk of haystacks, fog in ascent,
not where traffic sings its sexless honking
can anyone mark the dim-out of frogs,
the dying off of dragonfly wingbeats.

I am pulled up — I levitate October tugged
away from the rat-doomed isle
clearing the water tanks and steeple tops,
held fast on course by Orion's glimmer,
the angry scorpion tail fast behind me.
With leaves and dust I fly to the lake shore,
to the pumpkined heart, the base and the root,
the earth I touch as pole and battery.

I love this village, though it loves not me;
remember it, though it erases me.
I mark in my life, how I bear and remember
Octobers, and I know that a year is judged
by how it dies in these treetops: if it is burned
to cloud the eyes of men, or if it lies, burst
red in its full regale, waiting for snow,
        and the worms
and the spring, yes, to feed a new sun!

Earth, I am an ochre sheet of your leaves,
leaves more frequent than men in my lines,
leaves more fertile than mothers can be, leaves,
red, yellow, ambitious, how you have crept!
Leaves who have chilled my undraped lovers at night,
leaves sharing graveyard solemn caress with my lips,

<14>

leaves recurring everywhere to say their red gossip,
leaves for all I know returning again to this fall,
   to this place, still blushing to recount
   how lovers were spent in their bed,
   leaves forever spelling the name of lost love!

You names that rise to my lips on October nights,
   you sleep-thieving echoes of aspirant heart,
   rise from the sealed tomb of years, drag shroud,
   where no leaves chatter nor branches impede
   dead, in the track of stalking remembrance--you
   who wake me alone in my grave, grave bed to recall
     each passionate urge from green twig.

Each, each and all have grown red,
   defiant in the drugged fall,
denying parentage in terrible wind,
   nonetheless breaking free,
falling to my love in your high flame,
   red, then wet,
moist in your sombre dissent, then dry, then dead,
then in my hand the brown dust
   that a seed should come to,
a leaf forever spelling the name of lost love!

<16>

ANNIVERSARIUS IV

THE ISLAND

The island beckons. Trees strain
to hold their harvest, tug back
as chilling wind seduces leaves
to snap and break away.
My leaf is not wanted —
too strange for its fellows,
its angles odd, its song
too weird and wordy,
too full of bats and moonlight.
The island beckons. A hawk,
descending, tears me free —
umbilical to oak is severed
as tender talons seize me.

<17>

Yet even raptor releases me:
my planes are wrong —
oblique, I tumble windward,
touching down nowhere,
solo among enlisted legions,
not fitting any leaf pile.
No hand will hold me —
the island beckons.
I land upon the pavement.
I sense I belong here,
that I will give this crystal place
my autumn madness.
Decked in October
  the island beckons.
Others will come!

1968-1969, Edinboro/New York; rewritten 1995

<18>

WITH POE,
ON MORTON STREET PIER

Sunset at the Manhattan piers: gray-black,
the iron-cloaked sky splays vortices of red
into the Hudson's unreflecting flow.
Blown west and out by a colorless breeze,
the candle of life falls guttering down
into a carmine fringe above oil tanks,
a warehoused cloud of umber afterglow,
hugging the scabrous shore of New Jersey,
a greedy smoker enveloped in soot.

To think that Poe and his consumptive Muse
stood here in April, Eighteen Forty-Four,
his hopes not dashed by a rainy Sunday —
an editor thrice, undone, now derelict,
author of some six and sixty stories,
his fortune four dollars and fifty cents.
Did he envision his ruin, and ours?
Did his eureka-seeking consciousness
see rotted piers, blackened with creosote?
Did rain and wind wash clean the Hudson's face,
or was it already an eel-clogged flux
when he came down the shuddering gangplank?

Who greeted him? This feral, arched-back cat,
fish-bone and rat-tail lord of the landing?
Did he foresee the leather'd lonely wraiths
who'd come to the abandoned wharf one day
in a clank-chain unconscious parody
of drugged and dungeon-doomed Fortunato
and his captor and master Montresor?
He gazed through rain and mist at steeple tops,

<19>

warehouse and shop and rooming house — to him
our blackened brickwork was El Dorado.
He needed only ink to overcome
the world of Broadway with his raven quills —
Gotham would pay him, and handsomely, too!
Did the lapping waters deceive him thus —
did no blast of thunder peal to warn him
that this was a place of rot and rancor?

The city shrugs at the absolute tide.
I am here with all my poems. I, too,
have only four dollars and fifty cents
until tomorrow's tedium pays me
brass coins for passionless hours of typing.
I am entranced as the toxic river
creeps up the concrete quay, inviting me,
a brackish editor hungry for verse,
an opiate and an end to breathing.

Beneath the silted piles, the striped bass spawn,
welfare fish in their unlit tenements.
A burst of neon comes on behind me,
blinks on the gray hull of an anchored ship —
green to red to blue light, flashback of fire
from window glaze, blinking a palindrome
into this teeming, illiterate Styx.

The Empire State spire, clean as a snowcap
thrusts up its self-illuminated glory;
southward, there's Liberty, pistachio
and paranoid in her sleepless sunbeams,
interrogated nightly, not confessing.
It is not too dark to spy one sailboat,
passing swiftly, lampless, veering westward;
one black-winged gull descending to water,
immersing its quills in the neon mirror.

<20>

Now it is dark. Now every shadow here
must warily watch for other shadows
(some come to touch, to be touched, but others —)
I stay until the sea chill shrivels me,
past the endurance of parting lovers,
beyond the feral patience of the cat,
until all life on legs has crept away.

Still, I am not alone. The heavy books
I clasp together, mine and Edgar Poe's,
form a dissoluble bond between us.
Poe stood here and made a sunset midnight.
Poe cast his raven eyes into this flow
and uttered rhymes and oaths and promises.
One night, the river spurned his suicide.
One night, the river was black with tresses,
red with heart's blood, pearled with Virginia's eyes,
taking her under, casting him ashore.
One night, he heard an ululating sob
as the river whispered the secret name
by which its forgetful god shall know him,
his name in glory on the earth's last day.

— New York, October 20, 1970,
revised 1984, 1993; rewritten in 1995

<21>

TWO AUTUMN SONGS

1

Now Autumn chills the treetops and the red flare
of my October is the herald of new deaths,
exciting yellow plummets, ultimate green embraces,
consummate past tenses, dying chlorophyll,
   and so, love,
and I join flamboyant divers, break with the past
   of my sustenance,
   and so, love.
I rise from the summers of deep forgetfulness.
Inside my book the lovers have grown thin and dry.
   They crumble at my touch, my tongue
   finds not the lips nor flush of loin,
   but breaks from them decay's red ash,
   dust on the earth that all may walk upon.

2

Come that downward plummet of the world
and the stone gray sun's last sigh,
somewhere I will be waiting at the end,
be time or age or death the house of my
endurance, I am assured of biding you.
For in the waning orbit of your life, I am
that one and only who loving you
more than yourself, will be left by you;
   but with some gravitation
more divine than will I watch your ellipse
fade, and spend my scant affections
as the dying sun warms with his own
last fire the fleeting earth.

— October 1969, New York

<22>

ANNIVERSARIUS VII

LET WINTER COME

I have been here a quarter century —
now let me rest! let my contrary self
be silent this once — this year
no fancy from my leafy quill.
The lake will eat leaves without my lines;
the unacknowledged cold drops to the bone
from equinox whether or not
an anthem welcomes it.

Hear me, friend: I will not send you dead trees,
the frost no longer paints me orange.

<23>

I dodge the four winds' summons, evade
the draft of winter's war, refuse
to slurry down autumn with napalm frost.

My pen is dry.
Whole forms no spring can disinter
scream past me into shallow graves —
leaf-flake to vein to dust,
love springs from vernal lust
to tumble-leaf forgetfulness.
With summer gone, the past
is verdigris and peeling rust
a boneyard of false embraces
and terrified flight —

I shall be silent,
sliding down autumnless to snow,
ghostless on sainted All Souls' Eve,
sans pumpkins and tilted corn,
hymnless on harvest feast, chiding
the moon in slug-down count to twelfth-
month solstice and caroling.

Let winter come,
if it must.
I grow old in these leaves, like an old
mattress this ground has humored me.

The Muse of the acorn
is baffled by my silence.
What is there to sing?
I walk by their houses, whom I love.
I watch them fold into the shadows
until the blinkout freezes me.

<24>

Now I have nothing to say.
Why, leaves, do you follow me,
cling to my shoes and trouser cuffs,
skitter across the bridge before me,
laugh at my failed romance, shiver
me in this single bed and book?

Poor leaf, do you wonder
I will not write of you?
You know me too well, you know
at the end I will not scorn to love you
though I protest tonight.
The tree that bore you
knows I will come to lean on it,
waiting for dawn in the lake-edge snow.

Bereft of leaf and lover we'll watch
as lying Venus casts her pall on ice.
Why write a song that no one will hear,
love poems that make their object
    run for the horizon?

Leave me, autumn! Silence, winds!
Abandon, birds, these wretched trees!
Here are the pen, the ink, the paper,
    the empty virgin expanse —
    the lines pulling me like magnets —
No! no! I have nothing to say —
I will not write this poem.

— *1972, New York; revised 1983, 1995*

<25>

I PERSIST IN GREEN

Here on this hill there was no blossom time.
Though all was green, no nectar bee went forth
to fetch his fellows for a harvesting.
The scavengers give me a bleak report,
avoid my limbs where neither fruit nor nut
nor even bitter berries fall to ground.
I wait, still green with poetry, still wrapped
this autumn in dreams of Eden's April.
I am denied the killing kiss of frost —
one of a kind, I must stand sentinel,

watching as all the other trees go gray,
stripped bare by teasing wind, their naked arms
a stark and spindly silhouette on clouds.
I listen to their brittle colloquy,
see through and beyond their herded huddling
the universe their summer glyph concealed.

The sun and stars have dragged the fruiting urge
to climes unseen, but I persist in green.
I wave my rustling, needled arms aloft,
exude a youthful fragrance, still let the sap
fill my old head with springtime dalliance.

I call in thousands of lonely sparrows,
converse with the unwanted beggar birds,
invite the nests of those who stayed behind,
ignoring the season's bleak intelligence.
Stay here, hawk-free and sheltered from the storm!
Our wormless winter, though lean as a bone,
is spent with friend and feather, not alone.

<26>

Should I envy the others — the red-flagged
maples, the golden willows, browning oaks?
Is nakedness to wind more honest, then?
Are roots more wise when bald of leaves above?

Look at those tattered and abandoned nests!
Read me — my rings can prove and testify
whose way of wint'ring is the better lot!

The slanting, icy sun accuses me,
fringes with frostbite my emerald crown.
No fevered red, no golden rash, no brown
of rust has marred me — let winter come!
Should I not fear the hubris-humbling flood,
the thrust of fire from angry thunderers?

<27>

Am I too boastful of my isolate,
self-centered endurance? No god has come
to topple me, no hatchet-man has climbed
to mark or cut me for cabin timber.

One thing there is that can make me tremble:
I have dreamt of the distant mountain range,
of hill beyond hill, and peak surmounting
peak, of crags an eagle dares not soar to,
of nameless unscaled turrets of granite.
On each there grows, as here, an untamed tree,
alone and defiant, giant and free.

I dream, too, of an alpine wanderer,
whom I have ever loved, though never seen.
I bloom before the Passionate Stranger,
whose words bring news of my exiled brethren;
I bear strange fruit that falling, speaks and sings
new wonders to the astonished sparrows.
Then I blush red and amber and ochre,
shrugging my leaf-fall in a cry of joy.

We hold a strange communion, traveler
and tree. Kings of our kind, we cannot bow,
but lean into the wind together, twined
till cloth and bark, flesh and root-tap mingle.
To him, I make the wind that is Autumn;
to me, he makes the hope that will be Spring.
Holding dead leaves in one another's palms,
we are the sum of blossom, pollen, seed and fruit.
We are the thing we loved, the self made whole
by loss of self in love's surrendering.

— *December 1973, Edinboro, Pennsylvania;*
rewritten in 1995

<28>

OCTOBER RECKONINGS

The seasons merge: from a sunless autumn,
to winter without snow. What month it is,
is anybody's guess. The yard goes dry,
the grapes cut back turn brittle; brown
sparrows tramp noisily for last desserts
on arbor top; ailanthus arms take on
a sere and whiter hue, no trace
of tropic sprays of verdure now, no flag
like native trees, of where the green had been
(perhaps they migrate and plant themselves
on other trees!) It is a time
of reckonings, to heap the harvest up
and count each gain against its cost.

Little it means to measure what was lost —
the never had's a finer feast to sup.
It has a wine (whoever sees
the cask forgets himself and imitates
its salty plaint) from where the grapes had been,
of tears and rust and vanities, no flag
sincere of deeds or worth, no brace
of reason's air; drinking us in it sprouts
its arrows from inside our hearts.
It speaks of love, its tendrils crown
arbors without leaves. What year is it?
All lonely autumns are alike
at winter's verge.

— December 19, 1976, New York

<29>

THE GRIM REAPER

Autumn, and none too soon for me.
Bitter blasts unshingle the trees
and scatter the birds — the diminution
to bone branch by gale's tooth.

Ave! I welcome you, Red Harvester
of yet another year! I kindle fire
and hold my midnight watch atop a hill.

Ave! for everything awaits you:
the arbor picked clean of fruit,
the willows decked in banners of gold,
the windfall of currency
   from the abundant oaks.

Ave! Great Reaper who takes a year of everything.
Great Reaper who grinds the present to dust,
Great Reaper the only god (the others no more
than barricades you sweep aside, leaf dunes)

I see you. Your eyes play through me as easily
as sight itself moves through these barren trees.
You have no face. Two flames from out
your hooded darkness acknowledge me.
The scythe on which the world-end hone
but lately sang is in your hand.

<30>

My time is not yet come, thrice hailèd one.
I too must reap. I too must count the census
of lost leaves. My song must satisfy
before your hand can take the sheaf.
This space, this interstice between
the solstices is safe. My time
is not yet come.

— *December 17, 1978, New York; revised 1981*

<31>

ANNIVERSARIUS XI

DEAD LEAVES THE EMBLEMS TRUEST

Autumn
    love the Autumn
would fill the earth with perpetual
Autumn;
    if I were rich enough
I'd follow Autumn everywhere/
Paint my home in Shelley's orange
  and brown and hectic red;
rub tincture of turning leaves
onto my own limbs to motley
  my skin into a panoply
  of hues; buy potted trees
and fill my darkened rooms with them,

<32>

inject them full of October
until I lay ankle deep in fallings

of pages more wrinkled and withered
and crisped and sere than poor Poe's

Spring
    I salute only as birth-of-death
Summer   its ripening
Autumn   the fruit
Winter   the ice-toothed bacchanal
    of rampant death

Dead leaves the emblems truest of what we are:
cut to a rasping skeleton by time,
best in our wormwood age,
most useful to our kind
when closest to verge of nothingness.

How wise you are, detached
    at last from your origins,
borne by a wind that will not betray you,
confident, sun-singed, beyond all pain,
surging toward heaven without an enemy
    to hold you back, assured of what
is written in your own veined hand —
that you are a particle of glory returning to god.

To *god*? What folly! like old men whose legs
cannot support them you tumble down in heaps.
You burn in hecatombs, boots crush you to dust;
you are composted until the merest speck of you
is salt for the cannibal taproots of Spring.

Magnificent folly! For what is there at the end
of a billion misled heartbeats but this putting on
of shrouds? Should we not deck ourselves as well

<33>

as the oak tree, as maples jubilant,
or triumph-touched in willow's gold?

I think I shall be Autumn's minister.
Instead of those hearts torn out for the Aztec god,
I offer up a basket of leaves; instead of blood
upon the butcher block of Abraham I slay
a wreath of myrtle and laurel boughs;
upon the thirsty cross I nail a scarecrow Christ,
a wicker man with leaf-catch crown of thorns —

It was the cross itself that died for us
    the man a nobody
        a tree-killing carpenter

And folly still!
    The lightning limns the bare branch elm
    The hollow trunk howls thunder of its own
        to oust the thunder of god
The slaked storm passes, the fire-striped
        masts of the earth-ship stand.

Ear to the tree trunk, I hear the echo
        of the storm, the last tree-
        spoken words:
            I bring you glad tidings —
            There is no god.

There is no god, and when trees speak
the storm falls back in silence, shamed
    and reprobate.
There is no god, and when trees speak
    you kill them for the truth
    you cannot bear.

           —June 14, 1981, Madison Square Park,
           New York City, rev. 2011.

<34>

GREEN THINGS ARE MELANCHOLY

Some say these winter hills are sad.
I think not so.
      Gray bark and snow
are just the world in homespun clad,

plain and simple, honest and bare
to branch and root,
      dry underfoot —
these are the ones who do not dare

rebellion or unruly flight.
The withered sleep,
      the dream they keep,
to them is wisdom's light.

Green is the melancholy hue:
seedling and twig,
      blossom and sprig,
rioting upward, askew,

climbing aslant in May's folly
following one
      devious sun—
how can this be melancholy?

Just ride the suicidal breeze:
seed-spewing trees,
      lecherous bees,
the wingèd birds' hypocrisies —

<35>

These are false harbingers of joy.
What use are they?
        Their vernal play
is but a manic's fevered ploy.

Wait till the frost arrives — what then?
The birds fly south.
            The wizened mouth
Of fruit and flower saddens men

With bitter kisses youth should scorn —
The chill and numb
            chrysanthemum
as blanched and dry as ravaged corn —

The maples shorn have been undone —
The barren vine
        a twisted line
of snake embracing skeleton

The lily stalks are cripple canes.
The pale worm flees
            the apple trees.
A gray mist fills the lanes.

Green is the hue
        betraying you
for a handful of earth
        or a moment of dew!

— *December 17, 1978, New York;*
revised 1981, 1993, rewritten in 1995

<37>

ANNIVERSARIUS XIII

AUTUMN PORTENTS

Nights
lengthening
world
turning the corner of
dusk light entropy —
tip-of-tongue Autumn
(my budding anniversarius):
root-clogged Manhattan
perched at leaf flood,
drinking its one
last sunset before the burst —
sunspot and solar flare
leaf-veining the sky.

A red tide gathers
off Lebanon's shore,

leaf turn into October's war.

— October 1, 1982, New York

<38>

TWO FULL MOONS IN OCTOBER!

This double-mooned month
  full on the first
  doomed to be
  calends full again
in leaf-smoke aureole —
a double dose
of werewolf attacks,
crank cramped women,
a lunatick/tock calendar
assassinearthquake

<39>

poison pill panic
3-D knife-kill cinema

two madhouse moons
tipping the Libra scale

October
burning its leaves at both ends.

— October 4, 1982, New York

<40>

THE ORIONID METEORS

Nightfall of Orionids, fireworks unseen
above a city swathed in rain clouds,
stones torn from Haley's comet path
spice-frying ionosphere to carbon ash,
iron melting, quartz cracking and glowing red —
light show for the unseen Seer, dimming Aurora
at edge-slice dawn of yellow sun.

Spacefall of Orionids in October night!
Rock slabs from shattered worlds, gleaming in red,
blue-white and gold, amber and purest white,
turning in windless space and sunless careen,
each one a messenger of million-year age —
What were you? tombstone or cornerstone,
keystone or sidewalk slab? What kind of men
shaped you or mortared your intransigence
into a form of conscious will? What hands
took chisel and wrote a poem on you?

Leaf-fall of Orionids,
toss-tumble to hungry sun,
burn in the name of the world
that shed you, deciduous,
maple and oak and willow —
petrified!

—June 8, 1985, The Abode, New Lebanon, NY

<41>

OCTOBER IS COMING!

1
Listen! There is a sudden pause
between my words and the surrounding
silences: no breeze, no hum
of street lamps, no tread of tire —
even the birds have missed a beat.
It is the first self-conscious tinge
of maple leaf red, the first
night-chill of the season.
It is the caesura of equinox —
it whispers a prophecy:
October is coming.

It will not be like any other October.
You will be torn from the things that bind you.
You will follow a strange wind northward.
You will tread the edge of glaciers
  and blush with the iron tinge of destiny.
You will come to earth in a strange place
where you will be known as a leaf from an alien tree
  and be feared for it,
where you will seek the tongue-touch of another
  rasping exile — and find it.

Not for you the comfort of old trees,
  old branches, old roots —
now at last the buoyant freedom of the nearly
  weightless,
the eyrie-view above pine-tops, eddied above
  rain troughs and lightning rods,
bird-free,

<43>

drifting ghostlike and invisible on graveyard mound,
grazing the cheeks of grievers, pausing
    upon the naked backs of lovers,
tracing the mysterious barricades between
    the kingdoms of strays,
colliding with children in their chaotic play-

Hearing at night with brittle ears the plaintive sea,
    the wearing away of shoreline,
the woeful throb of the requiem of whales,
the madrigal of feeding gulls, the thrust beat
    of the albatross in its pinioned flight,
the hideous slurring of squids,
the inexorable gnashing of the machinery of sharks —

Mute, passive, dumb as a dead leaf
    you shall hear them all —

You shall move among the avalanche of first snow,
amazed at the shattering of perfect ice,
its joyous crystalline tone as it falls,
the utterly new dimension of its remaining,
endlessly crushed and compacted and moved,
singed to a fog and sublimed away
as if it had never been, while you
still lay like an old coat in a hamper —
grayer, crisper, more decrepit than ever.

And you suspect your lingering immortality-
a leaf, a brittle parchment that no one can read,
a shard, a skeleton of cellulose,
a thread, a string, a lichen roost, a bird-nest lining,
a witness of ever-advancing decay and assimilation,
by becoming nothing, becoming everything.

<44>

2

Yet this is such an insubstantial fate.
I can think of it now in the context
    of this human frame,
hands to write it, lips to speak it
    as transcendental prophecy.
Not only the dead but the living
can pass to this realm beyond matter.
All who have lived or ever will are there already
but only one in a thousand suspects it.

Why, then, do I crave for touching,
for arm-enfolding tenderness on winter nights?
Why do I ache for the line of a slender neck,
a moist surrender, the firmness of flesh,
the drumbeat sonnet of another's heart
loud in my ears, the harmony
of pacing my breath to another's breath,
falling limbs entwined into a trusting sleep,
or waking first and thanking the gods
for this wall of life between me and uncertainty?

I do not know, except that love
is the fluid of the Muses,
the enhancer of meaning, chariot of purpose,
that one plus one is not two
    but infinity,

that entropy, this modern malaise
    of the wasting leaf
is the false side of the coin of nature —
base metal welded to hidden gold.

<45>

3
Listen! October is coming!
It will not be like any other October.
You will be torn from your ease and comfort
by the one who loves you. You will follow
a strange wind northward, not as surrender
to an autumn urge, but as a warrior
for Spring. Glaciers will shudder back
at the green fringe of your beard. Your smile
will make strangers trust you, ask to know
what manner of tree sends youthful emigrants —
even the dry-leaf exiles will stir at your arrival.
You shall not pass the winter in random flight,
    nor cling to the steeples and chimney-tops.

Not for you the graveyard and its lying testaments,
not for you the vicarious touching of lovers and losers —

All shall know you and say of you:
Here is the one who loves and risks all.
You shall not heed the devious sea
and the night-call of Neptune's ravenous hosts.
The owl, the raven, the whippoorwill,
    the squirrel, the cat, the sparrow
shall teach you the ways of their defiance of season,
their hidden thrust for continuance.

Boisterous, active, strident as a new tree
    you shall take root again,
defying the shadow master of winter,
    the devil of frost,
refusing to yield one leaf to the ache-long nights.

And you rejoice in your numbered mortality,
in love, at risk of happiness for a single embrace,
at risk of loss and denial, too —
but knowing it and caring not.

<46>

A love, an eye, a heart, a hand,
a witness to ever advancing hope,
one to the power of infinity —
one plus a fraction, approaching,
but never reaching, duality.

4
Which shall it be? This orient autumn
or this renascent spring? This painless slide
into the lush oblivion of ash, or wing beat
in Daedalus flight to a promised star?

I only know that October is coming.
It will not be like any other October.

— September 1985, Providence, RI

<47>

THE STATE VERSUS AUTUMN

Resolved: For the sake of decency
and the order of the land,
the Congress hereby abolishes
the unwanted month of October...
No more Octobers ever?
Has the Society to Outlaw Gloom at last
succeeded in the Senate halls?
Has the Lobby Against Dead Leaves
banished arborial pollution?
Resolved: That the falling of leaves
disrupts the conduct of business,
distracts our children from their studies,
depresses the widowed and elderly...
We hereby outlaw deciduous trees.

How long, then, till the squad cars come
with their phalanx of armored cops,
handcuffing my corner sycamore,
chainsawing the neighbor's rowan tree,
tearing the vagrant maple from the street,
screaming with bullhorns for the ailanthus
to disperse from hillsides and parking lots,
interrogating runaway saplings all night,
wresting confessions from an effeminate birch?

The casualties will mount beyond reckoning,
the loss of leaves beyond count,
numbers too large for a superchip
or the chambered cranium of a C.P.A.

<48>

It's a conspiracy, of course:
the Moral Majority, the Vatican,
Jehovah's Witnesses, the Mormons,
an arm-in-arm league of Fundamentalists,
their hidden object a simple one:

Outlaw Halloween! They claim
the day is a Communist plot,
a pact of Satan and Hollywood,
Beelzebub and Publishers' Row.
A turning of innocent youth from God,
an anarchist's field day,
a sadist's orgy of pin-filled apples
and candies injected with LSD.

On Halloween, the faithful complain,
you cannot tell who the homosexuals are.
On Halloween, too much of the world
tilts to the literal Devil's side.

The bill has amendments, of course.
It will be a felony to serve up Poe
to those of tender and gullible age.
Horror books and movies? Goodness, no!
Bradbury's tales, and Brahms' autumnal tones,
LeFanu and Bierce, Blackwood and James,
Hawthorne and Derleth, Leiber and Bloch,
a whole amendment proscribing Stephen King,
real or pseudonymous, and prison for life
for reading Lovecraft and his protégés!

<49>

And so, a stitch in time is made.
September's harvest blinks
   to winter's barren hills.
A month of mail will never be delivered.
Today a marshal comes up to my desk,
tears page after page from my calendar.
Someone is blacking out words in the library books.
The date of my birth no longer exists.
These politicians mean business!

— September 1985/ October 1986, Providence RI

<50>

SON OF DRACULA

I was the pale boy with spindly arms
   the undernourished bookworm
   dressed in baggy hand-me-downs
   (plaid shirts my father wouldn't wear,
   cut down and sewn by my mother),
old shoes in tatters, squinting all day
for need of glasses that no one would buy.

At nine, at last, they told me
   I could cross the line
to the adult part of the library
those dusty classic shelves
which no one ever seemed to touch.

I raced down the aisles,
   to G for Goethe and *Faust*
     reached up for *Frankenstein*
at Shelley, Mary
      (not pausing at Percy Bysshe!)
     then trembled at lower S
      to find my most desired,
      most dreamt-of —
Bram Stoker's *Dracula*.

This was the door to years of dreams,
   and waking dreams of dreams.
I lay there nights,
the air from an open window chilling me,
waiting for the bat,
the creeping mist,
     the leaping wolf
the caped, lean stranger.

<51>

Lulled by the lap of curtains, the false
sharp scuttle of scraping leaves,
I knew the night as the dead must know it,
waiting in caskets, dressed
in clothes that no one living could afford to wear.

The river town of blackened steeples,
    vile taverns and shingled miseries
had no appeal to Dracula. Why would he come
when we could offer no castle,
no Carfax Abbey, no teeming streets
from which to pluck a victim?

My life — it seemed so unimportant then —
lay waiting for its sudden terminus,
its sleep and summoning to an Undead
sundown. How grand it would have been
to rise as the adopted son of Dracula!

I saw it all:
how no one would come to my grave
to see my casket covered with loam.
My mother and her loutish husband
would drink the day away at the Moose Club;
my brother would sell my books
    to buy new baseball cards;
my teachers' minds slate clean
    forgetting me as they forgot all
    who passed beneath and out their teaching.

No one would hear the summoning
    as my new father called me:
Nosferatu! Arise! Arise! *Nosferatu*!

<52>

And I would rise,
  slide out of soil
    like a snake from its hollow.
He would touch my torn throat.
The wound would vanish.
He would teach me the art of flight,
the rules of the hunt
  the secret of survival.

I would not linger
  in this town for long.
One friend, perhaps,
  I'd make into a pale companion,
another my slave, to serve my daytime needs
(guarding my coffin,
  disposing of blood-drained bodies) —

as for the rest
of this forsaken hive of humankind,
I wouldn't deign to drink its blood
  the dregs of Europe

We would move on
  to the cities.
The pale aristocrat and his thin son
  attending the Opera, the Symphony,
  mingling at Charity Balls,
Robin to his Batman,
  cape shadowing cape,
  fang for fang his equal soon
    at choosing whose life
      deserved abbreviation.

<53>

A fine house we'd have
   a private crypt below
      the best marbles
         the finest silk, mahogany, brass
         for the coffin fittings
Our Undead mansion above
   filled to the brim with books and music...

I waited, I waited —
   He never arrived.

At fifteen, I had a night-long nosebleed,
as though my Undead half had bitten me,
drinking from within. I woke in white
of hospital bed, my veins refreshed
with the hot blood of strangers.

Tombstones gleamed across the hill,
lit up all night in hellish red
from the never-sleeping iron furnaces.
Leaves danced before the wardroom windows,
blew out and up to a vampire moon.
I watched it turn from copper to crimson,
     its bloating fall to treeline,
     its deliberate feeding
   on corpuscles of oak and maple,
      one baleful eye unblinking.

A nurse brought in a tiny radio.
One hour a night of symphony
was all the beauty this city could endure —
I held it close to my ear, heard Berlioz'
Fantastic Symphony: the gallows march,
the artist's Undead resurrection
amid the Witches' Sabbath —
my resurrection. I asked for paper.

<54>

The pen leaped forth and suddenly I knew
that I had been transformed.
I was a being of Night now. I was Undead
since all around me were Unalive.

I saw now what they could not see,
walked realms of night and solitude
where law and rule and custom crumbled.
I was a poet.
I would feed on Beauty for blood,
   I would make wings of words,
      I would shun the Cross of complacency.
A cape would trail behind me always.

— *1986, Providence, RI; revised 1990; rewritten 1995*

<55>

NOT YEARS ENOUGH

How many autumns more? I cannot guess.
How slowly thirteen moons go rolling by,
how achingly the thirty dozen days
count off the torn inked sheets of calendar.
Life wrinkles silently, by phases imperceptible
the skull and bones show through the flesh.
More than the other signs of passing
the shelf of unread books accuses me —
not years enough to read them all!
And all those books unwritten, languages
to learn the lilt of, music to shape
beneath the independent fingers —
millions of words and thousands of melodies.
No matter what, the end must come
before the final page is writ, the coda sung.
Composers dreaded to start their Ninth
of symphonies, but trembled all the more
when the Ninth was done, behind them.
How many symphonies would they eke out
before the unrelenting knock of Fate?

If only Sleep, that dark-eyed panda,
were less the brazen thief — if only dreams
could quicken the long drear nights
with more than a passing vision.
I do not need to dream-quest Mt. Yaanek —
a quiet study would do, a reading lamp,
a chair and a sturdy book. My ka,
my lazy double, my astral body
can lounge on a hammock with a Dickens novel,
lean over calligraphy in a Ming gazebo,
or browse through the night-locked Athenaeum.

<56>

Never too late to learn the names of trees,
of sleeping birds and withered flowers,
the *Three Kingdoms'* heroes, the ladies
and lovers of *The Story of the Stone*.
Or maybe I'd walk with book in hand
barefoot in graveyard, a midnight reader
of horror tales, an epic reciter.

<57>

I'd make the dead listen to the *Faerie Queene*,
count on their fingers the knights and Moors
of the endless *Orlando Furioso*,
wear them out with the embracing lists,
the straw that stuffs the *Song of Myself.*
Maybe my eyes would retrace Shakespeare.

But this is Autumn: lamp-dousing time
for my waking self, long nights sliding
to the gravity of solstice, dead leaves
like pages escaping me unreadable.
Ah! *War and Peace* requires another reading;
Gormenghast requires slow delectation;
I want to read all Cooper's novels again
in parallel with all Scott's *Waverly* tales;
read Greek and Runic verse aloud,
along with forty years (count them!)
of *Mighty Thor* comics. How many operas
have I heard without the libretto before me;
how many Schubert songs just grazed
my consciousness without the poems there?
Projects unending to attend to,
not years enough to read them all,
not years enough to count them!

— *October 31, 1987, Providence-New York,*
revised 1990, 2011

<58>

THE SAILOR AND THE OAK NYMPHS

Oak with its roots in core of iron,
lava-tipped fingers reaching to magma,
ancient beyond the reckoning of sun,
brown as the acorn egg that bore her,
branches tightened, taut as muscles
boles a gnarl of screaming faces
  echoes of strange births
  and even stranger lovers.

Her skin bears scars:
 the nettling name of some boy,
the pen-knifed initials of lovers
who long ago subsumed
   into the blur of humus,
the signature of a deeper attack,
knife-thrust of a drunken sailor
who slashed at her one moon-mad night,
breaking through bark to cambium.

She was a long time healing,
but years before the gashes stitched
to spiderlines

they found the man in a nearby wood
  anonymous cadaver
  throat slit by self
  or by an unknown hand.

Knowing this oak,
I know how he came to be there,
I need but taste the tannin
of my October cup, but close
my eyes to see the tale unravel:

<59>

First came the virgin girl,
the gentle Amaltheia,
the tender one who lured him
before the tavern door,
offered him kisses, promised
to walk with him
in slanted light of the forest.

He waited not far from the bleeding oak.
The fair one broke her promise.
He cursed her, wished for the warmth
   of the familiar dives,
   the hot wet swallow
   of burning whiskey.

And then a lusty nymph appeared,
red-lipped in leather,
a slut who said her name was Jo,
   or Io, or some such thing.
This Io was inexhaustible,
fulfilling his every fantasy,
urging, then teasing,
then turning to mockery

of his all too human manhood.
Failing to please her,
he rolled away from her,
drifted into an angry stupor.
He lay half-dressed,
disheveled, undignified,
not hearing the flight of Io,
the leaf-crunch arrival
   of the barefoot hag,
the autumn crone, oak-born
Adrasteia, the unavoidable.

<60>

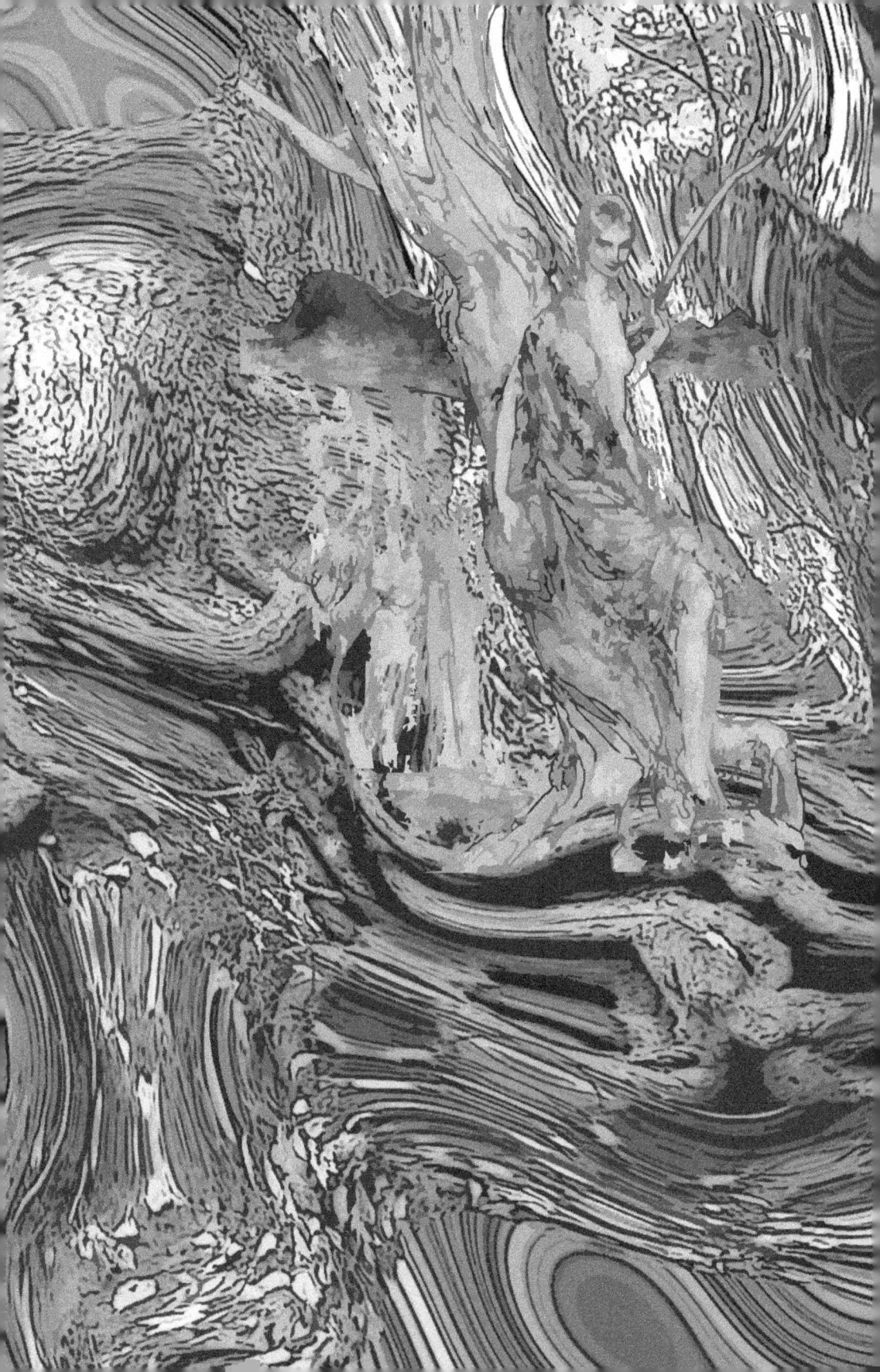

Before he could rise
from the cold-wet leaf bed,
she leaped on him,
    her bony knees on his shoulders
    breasts dry and pendant
        through tattered nightgown,
    nipples like withered twigs
    hair limp and gray
        and knotted with burrs,
her breath as she kissed him
the scent of apple rot,
the hint of something dead
turned up beneath wet leaves.

Her cracked voice whispered
the song the oak tree taught her:
of the hundred-handed slayers
  who sharpened knives in caves,
of the red-fanged worms
  burrowing up to find him,
of the arctic wind unleashed
  to follow him everywhere
  like a personal iceberg.

Then she was gone. He lay
beneath a tilted moon,
  a mocking Venus,
dry-mouthed and aching
with the bite of frost.

He found his pockets emptied,
wallet and coins,
greenbacks among the soggy leaves

<62>

his pocket knife,
his comb,
his fine-honed shaving razor
 already open
blade gleaming on a blood red banner,
the singing leaf of the oak tree.

— *October 31, 1987, Providence-New York,*
revised 1990

<63>

END OF THE WORLD

Not with a trumpet
  but a whisper. No angels
proclaimed the end. Prophets
with sandwich signs
 did not predict it.
No tea-leaf ladies
  or noted astrologers
knew that the end would come
at half-past eight
  in the morning.

It was a Monday,
  (of all days!)
catching them dressed
for their funerals.

Who would have guessed
that this October,
instead of leaves
the people turned
and blew away,
that gravity,
the faithful plodder,
would take a holiday?

First some commuters
on a platform in Connecticut
fell straight into a cloudless sky
trying to hook
  to lampposts and poles
with flailing arms.

<64>

Even the oversize stationmaster
was not immune,
hung by his fingertips
to shingled roof,
an upside-down balloon.
His wig fell down,
the rest of him
shot shrieking upwards.

Slumlords in Brooklyn
dropped rent receipts,
clutched hearts and wallets
as they exfoliated,
burst into red and umber explosions
and flapped away.

A Senator stepped down
from his bulletproof limo,
waved to the waiting lobbyist,
  (sweaty with suitcase
   full of hundreds)
only to wither to leaf-brown dust,
crumbling within his overcoat.

Stockbrokers adjusted their power ties,
buttoned their monogrammed blazers,
pushed one another from narrow ledge
falling from Wall Street precipice
into the waiting sky,
printouts and ticker tapes,
class rings and credit cards
feathering back down.

<65>

Bankers turned yellow,
wisped out like willow leaf
from crumpled pin-stripe,
filling the air
with streamers of vomit
as they passed the roof
of the World Trade Center.
The colors were amazing:
black women turned ivory,
white men turned brown and sere,
athletes swelled up
  to fuchsia puffballs,

Asians unfurled
  to weightless jade umbrellas.

Winds plucked the babies from carriages,
oozed them out of nurseries,
pulled them from delivery rooms,
from the very womb —
gone on the first wind out and upwards.

They filled the stratosphere
darkened the jet stream,
too frail to settle in orbit,
drifting to airless space.

They fell at last into the maw
of the black hole Harvester,
a gibbering god
  who made a bonfire
  of the human host
the whirling spiral of skeletons
a rainbow of dead colors
red and yellow and black and brown
  albino and ivory
parched-leaf skins a naked tumble.

<66>

The bare earth sighed.
Pigeons took roost in palaces.
Tree roots began
the penetration of concrete.
Rats walked the noonday market.

Wild dogs patrolled
  the shopping malls.
Wind licked at broken panes.
A corporate logo toppled
  from its ziggurat.
Lightning jabbed down
  at the arrogant churches
  abandoned schools
  mansions unoccupied

started a firestorm
a casual fire
as unconcerned
as that unfriendly shrug
that cleaned the planet.

                    — *October 31, 1987, Providence-New York*

<67>

THE OUTSIDER

Some say that spring
is made for lovers,
summer for marrying.
I do not know
those seasons:
I hastened on
when others mingled,
passed by alone
amid begetting.
I walked the city
for years not touching,
untouched and unafraid.

I am October.
I am conjured
of its red and yellow fever.
I am outlaw to life,
a thief of eyeballs,
citizen of a larger anarchy,
singer of dangerous
truths, peril to normalcy.

Little the world
loves pleases me.
Autumn-mad trees
mean more than palaces,
an austere tomb
more true than a cottage.

<68>

I love the earth —
love more
that vast black space
in which it rolls,
a lost marble.

I am the leaf that burns,
the candle that lights
  its own extinction,
sunset regarding itself,
sunlight spun round
the arc of infinity
until its end
sees its beginning.

I come out of the sea,
  walk sideways,
  write words
between the tide and shore.
I am the shape
  behind the randomness
  of stars,
the dream that fills
  the inkpot of Autumn,
the hooded Outsider
  who frightens you
  and laughs
then makes you laugh
at the absurdity of fear.

Will you stay indoors,
hoarding the apple harvest,
warming yourself
by a dead-tree fire?

<70>

Or will you join me,
fellow conspirator,
dance me between
the staves of symphonies,
roll in this new moon
blanket with me,

leaf-haired and cold
and laughing
giving up everything
to inherit all?
I am October.
  I wait at cusp,
  at equinox,
  at crossroads,

the far-off chant
unfettered wind
nowhere contained
    by walls,

the fire-fletched arrows
of burning Orionids,

the shape upon
  the leaf-strewn hill
that calls you
  and extends its hand,
the eyes in shadow
that will not let you sleep.

— *October 31, 1987, Providence-New York*

<71>

FRAGMENTS OF A HYMN TO RHEA, THE OAK TREE GODDESS

Earth-born Rhea   Queen of Oaks
Dryads' mistress and guardian
shelter and shade for the maidens three
who nursed the infancy of Zeus:
tender and virginal   dear Amaltheia
nubile and frantic   the dancing Io
withered and wild   dread Adrasteia

Oak in all your aspects   green-fired
in burst of spring   full-fruited
with pendant acorns   brown-limbed
and mourning on a hecatomb of leaves

A giant goddess   titanic oak
a sigil of your Titan origins

Still you echo   the thunder of shields
drumbeating spears   bare-shouldered Curetes
oak sons who guarded the infant god
baby in bird nest camouflage
stunned to silence by the tumult below

Your roots still plummet   to metals five
to mines of tin and lead and copper
veins of silver and fire-flaked gold

<72>

Mother of Gods and Sister of Titans
you it was who gave the stone to Cronus,
deceiving your cannibal husband
with granite wrapped in swaddling,
pretending to honor the infantophage,
blasphemer of the law of life.

It was you who raised the child in secret,
presented him as bastard cousin,
spawn of the lesser dwellers of ocean,
hostage cupbearer from trembling seas —
you who mixed the salt and mustard
into the nectar and watered wine,
you who stood by Zeus and whispered
words of courage and pride and waiting,
until the stupored Titan vomited,
disgorging the slimed Olympians
into the dark and cleansing river.

<73>

You were the lever that toppled your kind,
used wifely and cunning deceitfulness
to give the earth to the youngster gods.
And so you claimed a place in forest
took root and rest   welcomed the bird
the garland of clinging grapevine
zephyrs and rain   enduring the frost

sank roots when the moon was a baby,
saw it torn from the belly of ocean.
Then came the slant-browed hominids,
brutish but neither animals nor gods,
their first house built
in a lightning-scarred trunk,
first meal a windfall
of sweet brown acorns
nut-milk of your abundance.

Rhea, Rhea, Rhea! Rhea, Rhea!
Hear the downward drumbeat
Rhea, Rhea   Pan cry
and lion roar   trilled chant
of your assembled priestesses.
Unveil us your mysteries
O red-haired Titaness,
acorn-jeweled Goddess!

Five-fingered leaves —
what are you saying?
Is this mad chattering
for mere birds only —
this frantic signaling
sign language of the Dactyls —
the virile thumb
the pointing index
the impudent finger
oracular, the tiny one —

<74>

Are you repeating the wind
or inventing it¿
Are you teasing us up from apehood
with signs and mysteries¿

You are silent as Saturn
with its leaf-dust rings.
Your scrolls fall everywhere,
a diaspora of scriptures.

I come to you alone   at midnight
I offer you   a Druid handshake
a subtle drumbeat   a melody.
Your great eyes open in rippled bark.
You do not speak. You seem to sense
how men have toppled your ancient temples,
how forests are torn   birds dispossessed

You sleep again   but where your eyes
had studied me   the amber tears collect
the amber tears of Rhea

— November 3, 1987, Providence, RI

<75>

RUNAWAYS

I want to report a disappearance.
No, not exactly, not a person.
No, not a pet. Lost property?
What's missing isn't mine to lose,
    but it has certainly vanished.
The tree — the tree in front of my house
    is just plain gone.
Just yesterday I raked the leaves,
the first red flags of autumn.
The maple was there. I touched it,
traced with my hand its withered bark.
Today it's gone, root, branch and leaf.
Just a hole in the pavement,
a heap of gravel, a trail of clotted soil
down and around the corner.

Nothing disturbed my sleep.
No chain saw, crane or dynamite
chewed, toppled or fragmented
   my splendid shade tree.
I have no witnesses
except the baffled squirrels,
the homeless begging sparrows.
My neighbors seem not to notice —
    they're Mediterranean,
    prefer the sun and open space
    to my shady Druid grove.
I'll plant another tree, I guess,
though I'll be old before
its boughs can shelter me.

<76>

I wouldn't have come —
I would have borne the mystery alone —
except that — how do I say it? —
I think it's happening all over.
I notice trees. I walk the park,
maintain a nodding acquaintance with birds,
keep time by the blossoms,
the fruit, the rainbow of flame
when October exfoliates.
This morning the park
is missing three maples, two sycamores,
one each of elm and beech,
crab apple, peach and sassafras.
There's not a sign of violence:
no broken trunks, no sawed-off limbs,
no scorch of lightning.
Just holes in the ground,
deep channels where roots withdrew,
and where each tree had been,
a trail of gravel, worms and soil
    out of the park,
    onto the pavement,
    then — nothing.

Who's taking them, you ask?
You're the policeman,
   the missing persons authority.
I don't think anyone's taking them.
    I think they're leaving us.
Maybe they're going north to Canada.
Maybe they've had enough
of crime and dirt and corruption.
Maybe they'd like a little freedom,
a little peace and quiet.

<77>

You'd better investigate.
Imagine our city if this goes on:
Central Park a treeless dog run;
Park Avenue and Fifth two blazing corridors
of steam and sweat and screaming cabbies.

What would we be without our trees?
We brought them with us from Europe,
    our Johnny Appleseed inheritance.
For every wilderness we leveled
we came back planting, pruning,
framing our starry vision
with tamer treelines.

<78>

They civilize us, connect us
to the earth and the seasons.
Without them we are savages,
wolf eating wolf on the pavement,
buying and selling
with the handshake of scorpions.

Find them! Beg them to come back!
Ask them their terms!
Get the mayor to negotiate!
Promise them we'll do better.
We'll clean the streets again,
restore the parks and riverways.
We'll serenade the trees with Mozart,
outlaw rap and raucous riveting.
We'll do whatever it takes!
How could we go on without them,
leafless, treeless, barren and dead?

— *September 14, 1993, Boston to New Yor*

<79>

IN CHILL NOVEMBER

The leaves be red,
The nuts be brown,
They hang so high
They will not fall down.
    — Elizabethan Round, Anon.

The snow has come.
The leaves have fallen.
Long nights commit the chill
low sun and flannel clouds cannot disperse.
We walk the park, stripped now
    to mere schematics,
vision drawn out to farther hills
now that the forest is blanked
like flesh turned glass on X-ray negative.
These woods are sham so near the solstice,
play out a murder mystery of birch and maple.
The riddle is who's dead and who's pretending?
That witches' elm with clinging broomsticks—
    is it deceased or somnolent?
Which of these trees will never bloom again:
    A Lombardy poplar stripped by blight —
    A maple picked clean by gypsy moths —
    A thunder-blasted pedestal of ash —
    A moribund sycamore whose only life
        came in a few vain buds
        (growing like dead men's hair and nails,
        slow to acknowledge the rot below) ?
The ground's a color cacophony,
    alive, alive!
the treeline a study in gray and brown.

<81>

Now who can tell
   the bare tree from the dead,
   the thin man from the skeleton?
Which denizens of wood lot shed these leaves?
Which is a corpse? a zombie?
Which one is but a vermin shell?
Which treads the night on portable roots,
   festooned with bats,
      sinking its web of trailing vines
      into the veins of saplings?
Which stalwart oaks will topple,
which trunks cave in to termite nests?
How can we tell the living from the dead?

It's just the month: November lies.
   October always tells the truth.
You could no more fake
   the shedding of leaves
than simulate a pulse in stone.

Only the living fall in love,
only the living cry for joy,
only the living relinquish that month
in red and yellow shuddering!

The pines,
   those steeple-capped Puritans,
what price their ever-green?
Scrooge trees, they hoard their summers,
withhold their foliage,
refuse to give the frost his due.

Ah, they are prudent,
   Scotch pine and wily cedar,
   touch-me-not fir and hemlock.
They will live to a ripe old age
(if you can call that living).

<82>

Love! Burn! Sing! Crumble!
Dance! Wind! Fall! Tumble!
Into the wind-blown pyramid of leaves!
Spin in a whirling dust-devil waltz!
Leaf-pile! Treetops! Tramping on clouds!
Weightless, flying, red-caped October!

— *October 25, 1989, New York to Edinboro, Pennsylvania*

<83>

THE FENCE

Town fathers, what have you done?
Last night I returned
(I vowed — I made the lake a promise)
intending to tramp the lane of maples,
read with my palms the weary tombstones,
feast with my eyes the clouded lake,
lean with a sigh on founder's headstone,
chatter my verses to turtles and fish,
trace with my pen the day lily runes,
    the wild grape alphabet,
the anagram of fallen branches,
all in a carpet of mottled leaves.
The mute trees were all assembled.
The stones — a little more helter-
    skelter than before,
but more or less intact — still greeted me
as ever with their Braille assertions.
The lake, unbleached solemnity
    of gray, tipped up
and out against its banks to meet me.
All should have been as I left it.

Heart sinks. The eye recoils.
    My joy becomes an orphanage
    at what I see:
from gate to bank to bend
    of old peninsula,
    across the lot
    and back again,
sunk into earth
    and seven feet high
A CHAIN LINK FENCE!

<84>

Town fathers, what have you done?
Surely the dead do not require protection?

Trees do not walk.
    The birds are not endangered.
How have your grandsires sinned
    to be enclosed in a prison yard?
As I walk in I shudder.
    It is a trap now.
    A cul-de-sac.
I think of concentration camps.

For years, art students painted here—
    I hear the click of camera shutters,
    the scratch of pens,
    the smooth pastel caress,
    taste the tongue lick of water color,
    inhale the night musk of oil paints.
Poets and writers too,
    leaning on death stones,
    took ease and inspiration here,
    minds soaring to lake and sky.
At dawn, a solitary fisherman
    could cast his line here.

Some nights the ground would undulate
    with lovers
(what harm? who now would take
    their joy between two fences?)

The fence is everywhere! No angled view
can exclude it. It checkerboards
the lake, the sky, the treeline.

<86>

They tell me that vandals rampaged here,
   knocked over stones,
   tossed markers
     into the outraged waves.
Whose adolescents did this,
   town fathers?
         Yours.
Stunted by rock and stunned by drugs,
they came to topple a few old slabs,
struck them because they could not
   strike you.

<87>

Let them summon their dusky Devil,
rock lyric and comic and paperback,
blue collar magic, dime store demons —
            they wait and wait,
blood dripping from dead bird sacrifice
until the heavy truth engages them:

The dead are dead,
   magic is empty ritual,
      and stubborn Satan declines
to answer a teen age telegram.

Fence in your children, not our stones!

            — *October 25, 1989, Edinboro, Pennsylvania*

<88>

TO THE ARC OF THE SUBLIME

In nights beneath the stars,
   sometimes alone — sometimes
   with one I loved
      (in futile or secret urgency) —
I have outwaited
   the rise and fall of Scorpio,
     arc of its tail
       stinging the treetops.
I have traced the inconstant moon,
   the indecisive Venus;
   feel more assured
by the long, slow haul of Jupiter,
the patient tread of Pluto
   (whom they pursue
     in their frigid outer orbits
I cannot guess)

Such solitude,
   millennia between
     the fly-bys of comets,
perhaps is why
   they need so many moons,
why rings of ice
   encircle them like loyal cats.
It is lonely in space,
   far out
where the sun is merely
   a star among stars.

<89>

It is lonely in autumn.
   I sit in midnight woods.
A trio of raccoons, foraging,
   come up to me,
black mask eyes of the young ones
interrogating the first cold night,
   the unaccustomed noisiness
      of bone-rattle maple leaf
         beneath their paws.

How can I tell them
   these trees will soon be skeletons,
   the pond as hard as glass,
   the nut and berry harvest over?
These two are young —
   they would not believe me.
Their mother rears up protectively,
   smells me,   scents out
   the panic among the saplings,
   the smell of rust and tannin.

We share a long stillness,
   a moment when consciousness
   is not a passive agency.
Our sight invades the countryside,
   embracing everything —
   sleepers in beds in a concrete tower-
   earthworms entwining in humus rot —
goes up and out through the limpid sky,
   streaming past moon —
      — moon's lava'd seas —
out, out, to the arc of the sublime,
   tracing the edge of great Antares,
leaping to other galaxies unafraid.

<90>

(Let space expand as though the worlds
   still feared their neighbors!
Let miser stars implode,
   their dwarf hearts shriveling
      to cores of iron!)
We are the scourge of entropy.
   We sing the one great note
      through which new being
         comes out of nothingness.

Does it have meaning,
   this seed-shagged planet
      alive with eyes?
Is earth the crucible,
   sandbox of angry gods,
or is it the eye of all eyes,
   ear of all ears,
the nerve through which the universe
   acquires self-knowledge?

But these are weighty thoughts
   for man and mammal!
We are but blood and minerals,
   upright for an instant,
   conscious for but a moment,
   a grainfall of cosmic hourglass.
Yet I am not ephemeral:
   I freeze time,
      relive moments
         chronicle the centuries
   respeak Shakespeare,
      beat out the staves of Mozart,
         read the same books
         my forebears knew
      make of old words
         my wordy pyramid.

<92>

I am the one
   snapping the pictures of solar systems,
   sending myself
      an outside-in self-portrait.
I send my name and signature
   on bottles spinning past Uranus.
I am the one who asks, Is it worth it?
I who hear the X-ray wind reply, It is!
I am the one who would not stay in caves,
   I was discontent in the treetops.
I wanted to be bird and whale and rocket.

Ever, o ever more mortal now —
   — friends falling away like withered leaves —
still I find joy in this subliminal shrine of autumn.
My hand is full of fossil shells
   picked up from the lake shore rubble,
scallops enduring with the same rock faith
   (implicit minimum vocabulary):
I live, and the increase of my consciousness
   is the span of my life.

                    — *February 19, 1991, Providence, RI*

<93>

RING 2

THE CREEPERS

Halloween:
this is a night for paranoids,
the eve the living and dead
switch places, bonfires of souls
on top of every hilltop,
the night when life
walks tightropes over emptiness,
when autumn finally shrugs
its sorry burden of summer.

This night I am not flesh —
I am a web of ganglia,
a sensitive antenna
to every flow of energy.
I hear the droning wind,
hard-edged as needles,
wearing down stone
a micron at a serving.
I hear clouds scream
as they graze the metal edge
of shining office towers.

On the long cab ride homeward,
above the hiss of tires,
Tenth Avenue lampposts
utter a shrill soprano
of throbbing fluorescence.
Faceless figures shuffle by.
Tenements blur
to corrugated slabs
of half-seen brick,
yet I hear the whirring compressors
of a thousand air conditioners.

<97>

Latin songs bounce
off unlit pavement,
amorphous drumming
fills an empty warehouse.

Stop light: a clutch
of desperate hands
thrusts from a heap of coats
too old and shapeless
to issue more
than an extended palm

Ticked off in taxi meter dimes,
the pumpkin stroke arrives.
Midnight finds me
on Ninety-Fifth Street, my block
a corridor of feral eyes
gleaming in cellarways
(of all in this raucous city
only the cats know how to be silent!)

The trash can at the curb is rattling,
yard leavings jumbled with broken glass —
hagwig of brittle branch chattering,
a spear of broken mirror
peeling its silver backing
like a witch's unwanted reflection.
Sharp shards like frozen thunderbolts
make desolate wind chime clashes.
I dare not touch them —
they look hungry for a vein to slash!

Over my gloomy lintel
ivy sucks stone and air,
wrinkles with autumn wisdom,
spitting discarded leaves
as I pass in and under.

<98>

Ivy clings, too,
behind my bedroom.
Now, with my hyper ears,
I hear them rustling,
even, at times,
when there is no breeze.
The vine is an onramp for spiders,
a ladder for spotted snakes.

And now, as sure
as I hear it,
I know the ivy is listening.
It knows the keystrokes
of my typewriter
and can read each letter
by its distinctive click.
It even knows the scratch
of my pen, can mouth
my words as fast as I write them.
Hedera helix, I write —
the tiny voice titters back
"English Ivy! Our proper name!"

The egg of All Saints
cracks into dawn.
Vine laps the sunyolks,
tendrils exploring
new gaps in the masonry,
tilting vampire umbrellas
to the unsuspecting sun.

Smothering church and rectory,
carpeting the walls of the library,
cozying up the university halls,
the ivy horde is studying us
close up, from ape to rocket,
always averting those

<99>

underleaf eyes, those
sharp little teeth.

They mean to kill us slowly,
urban piranha reducing
brownstones to dust,
churches to rubble,
pigeons to skeletons —
insidious vines,
    lethal creepers!

—New York City 1974, rev. Weehawken 1996

<100>

LOVED ONES

Loved ones, the early dawn's
illusion-loves
seem still the finest
    though rippled dead
in the sea of years

Loved ones
    for whom mere sight
        was swooning,
    words full
of double, triple meaning,
eternal prospects,
    each falling into
    and out of
as certain and final
as the death of dinosaurs.

Loved ones
    afloat a haunted lake—
desperate trees,
    bone-dry bird nests
    a brambled heart
wintering on promises,
    utopias delayed
    in permafrost,
star-speckled night
    nerved with nebulas.
Yearning was more
    than having,
as every elm tree
    leaned with me
toward the absent beloved.

<101>

Loved ones
    outgrew those student days,
    subsumed to normalcy,
    sank like a stone to suicide,
    took up the faith.
The stars I named for my beloved
    shrug off their brightness, shamed
    at their worldly outcome.

Pursue the Beloved,
    a Sufi advises me.
It seems I hurled them skyward —
    Andromeda and Venus,
    Mars and Ganymede —
I am too fixed a star,
    my orbit limited
(evading black holes
    of death & depression,
wobbling a little
when some new planet approaches)

Loved ones
    escaped me:
the more they changed
the more immutable
the past became,
as what they were
and what I am
danced endlessly
in Autumn air.

—*New York City 1982, rev Weehawken 1996*

<102>

ANNIVERSARIUS XXX

AUTUMN ON MARS

for Ray Bradbury

On Mars the black-trunked trees are dense
with summer's crimson foliage.
When dry-ice autumn comes,
the oaks singe sickly green.
The land is a riot of airborne olive,
    chartreuse and verdigris,
green fire against a pink and cloudless sky.
The sour red apples go yellow sweet;
the wind-blanched wheat
    forsakes its purple plumage;
The Old Ones tie cornstalks in indigo bundles;
eyes flicker ghoulishly
    as they set out candles
        in carved-out green gourds.

Grandfathers warn their terrified children
of the looming, ominous blue planet,
roiled with thunderclouds and nuclear flashes,
that warlike, funeral-colored Earth
from which invaders would one day come,
decked in the somber hues of death,
withered and green like dead-pile leaves,
armed to the hilt with terrible weapons.

"I've seen them!" an elder asserts.
"They have two eyes, flat on their heads!"
Eye stalks wiggle in disbelief.
"They walk on two legs, like broken sticks!"
Multijointed leglets thump in derision.

<103>

"They speak in the animal octave,
        and they bark like krill-dogs."
The children shriek in red and purple.
"No way, Old One! Don't make us think it!
How can they talk without twinkling?"

"Their rockets go higher with every turn
        of our world around the life-star.
Earthers will come, thick on the ground
        like our thousand-year mugworms.
They will kill us, take our females captive,
burn our egg domes, eat our aphidaries!"
A fireball slashes the pink horizon.
Two hundred eye-stalks follow the arc.
"That might be one of their robots now!
Their probes are watching everywhere!"
Now fifty Martian youngsters scream,
shrieking in ultraviolet tones,
crab legs scattering in every direction.

The Old Ones smile in five dimensions,
sit down for a cup of hot grumulade
and some well-earned peace and quiet.
"It's not nice to frighten the young ones,"
the eldest muses, "but it wouldn't be autumn
without a little Halloween."

—*Halloween 1997, Providence, rev. 2002 Providence*

<104>

OCTOBER STORM

First night of the tenth month
a roaring storm hits town:
thunder from every side,
flash after cataclysmic flash
of blue-white lightning.
Transformers hum
and tempt the storm-stab,
birds hunch in branches,
cats dash
from on dry porch to another.
A set of solitary car lights passes,
distorted in sheets of rain,
taillights at the corner
like the haunted eyes
    of a carnivore
    who has just learned
    he is the last of his kind.
A siren signals a distant fire.

Lightning comes closer,
closest I have known in years.
I open the window,
smell of ozone,
watch as a nearby tree goes down,
raked by the fingernails
of a coal-black thunderhead.

I hold the new jade stone
on which a Chinese artisan
has carved my nascent Mandarin name:

<105>

Meng for the dream, the world in which all poets dwell —
Ch'iu for the autumn, my chosen province and capital —
Lei for the thunder of the mountain-striding storm.

I am the Dream of Autumn Thunder,
and this storm has called my name,
marked the day of my arrival
in the mysterious Middle Kingdom.

— October 1998, Weehawken

<106>

ON RECEIVING A GIFT OF BOOKS
IN EARLY OCTOBER

for Barbara Girard

The books are falling from the trees:
The Birds of Swan Point Cemetery
   still forest green
     with wide-eyed saw-whet owl
   pleading for continued foliage,
   months more of fat brown mice
   before the meager winter comes.

Here's Fraser's angry Wood King
   guarding his oak, his paranoia
     old as *The Golden Bough*,
   his staff and sword crossed,
   feet firm in the circle
     of abundant acorns
   not even the squirrels touch,
   fearing his wild words.

Not well concealed,
   that oily Aegisthus
     woos married Clytemnestra
   amid the thinning sycamores.
Troy is far off, the war is long.
He'll never come home, that
   ungrateful king, Agamemnon.

Now here's a well-used leaf,
   pock-holed already with frostbite,
red with laughter on top,
   brown with wisdom beneath,

<107>

I read at random:
　　"War is so savage a thing
　　　　that it rather befits beasts
　　　　　　than men —"
old friend Erasmus, your *Praise of Folly*

Here by the stately laurel
　　falls a wreath, twined round
　　with bands of gold, not far
　　from the supple columns
　　of the Athenaeum,
and the voice I first heard
in timeless tales of gods and heroes
spins out *Mythology* as truth
from the pen of Edith Hamilton —
o welcome leaves
　　from when the world was young.

Pruned branches piled for an *auto-da-fé*
　　sing and crackle: Here burns Voltaire,
　　Candide and his beloved Cunegonde.
Pangloss intones as flames roar up,
　　of the best of all possible worlds.

The Grand Inquisitor warms his hands,
is not amused as pine cones volley down,
needles of truth in evergreen pursuit,
crows mocking
as Trevor-Roper tells all
in *The European Witch-Craze*.

Some of this autumn fall is dangerous:
A Vindication of the Rights of Woman
a perennial leaf that will not wither,
brave Mary Wollstonecraft's
appeal to higher reason,
awaits its vindication still.

<108>

And here's *A History of the Primates*.
Are men descended from hairy apes?
   Just ask a woman.

Here's Forster's *Maurice*,
   a novel its author dared not publish,
   a brave, tormented book
   about a man who dared
      to be happy
      in his love for another man:
   I hold you, reticent English leaf,
   press you into my own heart's book
   and will not let the earth consume you.

And now the wind gusts out and upward,
ah, too many leaves to count now:
Jung and Proust,
Lawrence and Leopardi,
   so many books unread
   so many leaves one upon another,
         mountains of you like toppled libraries,
         pyramids of poems to kick through
   and millions more still waiting to fall!

—*October 1998, Weehawken. A poem written extemporaneously,*
      without plan, while examining, at random, a pile of
      books from a gift carton. The "random" effect was
      enhanced further by opening some of the books
      to random pages

<109>

AUTUMN SUNDAYS
IN MADISON SQUARE PARK

Stately old sycamores, sentinel oaks,
    fan-leafed gingko and noble elm,
year by year your patient quest for the sun
    has sheltered such madmen, squirrels,
birds, bankers, derelicts and poets
    as needed a plot of peaceful
respite from the making and sale of things.

<110>

Poe lingered here in his penniless woe.
    Melville looked up at a whale cloud.
Walt Whitman idled on the open lawn.
    (Sad now, the ground scratched nearly bare,
Fenced off against the depredating dogs;
    the fountains dry, while standing pools
leach up from old, sclerotic water mains.)

Four chimes ring for unattended vespers,
    no one minding the arcane call,
not the bronze orators exhorting us,
    not the rollicking hounds unleashed
in the flea-infested gravel dog-run,
    not the grizzled men in boxes,
so worn from the work of all-day begging

they're ready to sleep before the sun sets.
    A thousand pigeons clot the trees.
The northwest park is spattered with guano,
    benches unusable, a birds'
Calcutta, a ghetto a bloated squabs
    feasting on mounds of scattered crumbs,
bird-drop stalagmites on every surface!

<111>

Daily she comes here, the pigeon-lady,
    drab in her cloth coat and sneakers,
sack full of bread crusts, and millet and rice,
    peanuts and seeds from who-knows-where.
Still she stands, in the midst of offerings,
    until they light upon her shoulder,
touching her fingertips, brushing her cheeks

with their dusty, speckled wings, naming her
    name in their mating-call cooing,
luring her up to lofty parapets,
    rooftop and ledge, nest precipice
where, if she could fly, she would feed their young,
    guard their dove-bright sky dominion
from hawks, the heedless crowds, the wrecking cranes.

Across one fenced-in lawn the sparrows soar
    in V-formation back and forth,
as though they meant in menacing vectors
    to enforce the no-dog zoning.
Amid the uncut grass the squirrels' heads
    bob up, vanish, then reappear
as the endless search for nuts and lovers

ascends its autumn apogee. But here
    the squirrels are thin and ragged,
road-kill reanimated harvesters,
    tails curled like flattened question marks
as every other morsel offered them
    is snatched by a beak or talon.
Descending birds make calligraphic curves

<113>

as branches twine in spiral chase of sun.
     Nothing is safe from scavenging —
trash barrels tipped for aluminum cans,
     the ground beneath the benches combed
for roach-ends the dealers crush and re-sell
     to law clerks and secretaries.
Even the cast-off cigarettes are taken

by derelicts and nicotinic birds.
     Certain my notes are tracking him,
a storm-tossed schizophrenic darts away.
     Beside the World War's monument
(ah, naïve time, to conceive no second!)
     an Asian woman gardening
adds green and blossom to the shady ground

<114>

amid the place-names of trampled Belgium,
    forest and trench of invaded France.
(Not her war, certainly, not her heroes,
    yet her soft blooms, as from a grave
whisper the names of the now-dead warriors
    and sons who never come to read
of Ypres, Argonne and the barbed-wire lines.)

A welcome bookstall has opened its doors,
    as if to lure the passers-by
to read, to dream, beneath the timeless elms —
    but who can sit, immersed in book,
as suicidal leaves cascade, as hands
    shaking and thin, trade crumpled bills
for bags of bliss in crystal, crack or powder?

Is this the potter's field of shattered dreams?
    The copper arm of Liberty
once stood at the northern end of the square.
    The trees once soared. Now roots eat salt,
brush against steam pipes and rusted cable,
    cowed by courthouse, statues frowning,
Gothic and Renaissance insurance spires.

Only the branches, forgiving, forgetting,
    redeem this purgatory place.
A Druid stillness draws here at dusktime,
    squirrel and bird and runaway
equally blessed as the hot-ash sunset
    gives way to the neon-lit night,
city unsleeping beneath the unseen stars.

—New York City/ Weehawken/ Providence
1996/1998/2001

<115>

ANNIVERSARIUS XXXIV

SEPTEMBER IN GOTHAM

This is New York, and fall
   has caught us unawares.
From Palisade bus I view
   the gap-toothed skyline,
a forest whose tallest trees
   are suddenly missing.

In Gotham, they say,
strange breezes from the south
make certain elders remember
downwind from the death camps.
There is talk of stolen watches
from shops beneath the rubble,

<116>

the discovery daily
     of severed limbs.

Month's end, I walk all day
     in midtown,
with shoppers determined
to do something normal,
eat Szechuan lunch, browse
books, consider new software.
Like many others around me,
I pick things up from the counter,
     then put them back —
everyday urges seem so trivial.

There is not one note of music.
People keep stopping
     to stare nervously
     at the Empire State,
     like frightened squirrels
     in the shadow
     of a threatened sequoia.

The sycamores in Bryant Park
beam back the sun,
     an interrupted medley
     of overhanging clouds
     that pause, then part,
     then scud away.
Seedpods of honey locust fall,
curl brown like overdone toast
     on the pavement,
but the delicate leaves remain above,
     still adamant green.

<117>

It is not till night,
    till I turn the corner on Lexington
    and spy the dark hunched shell
    of the Gramercy Park Armory,
that I see the leaves of this autumn,
    its *feuilles morts*,
taped to treetrunks, walls and windows,
    tied to a chain link fence,
    row on row to the end of seeing,
flapping in rainstorm, tattered, tearing,
soon to be ankle deep in the gutter —

these album-leaves of anguish
burst forth with human colors —
faces brown and pink and salmon,
oak and ash and ebony,
the rainbow of human flesh,
    of eyeflash —

<118>

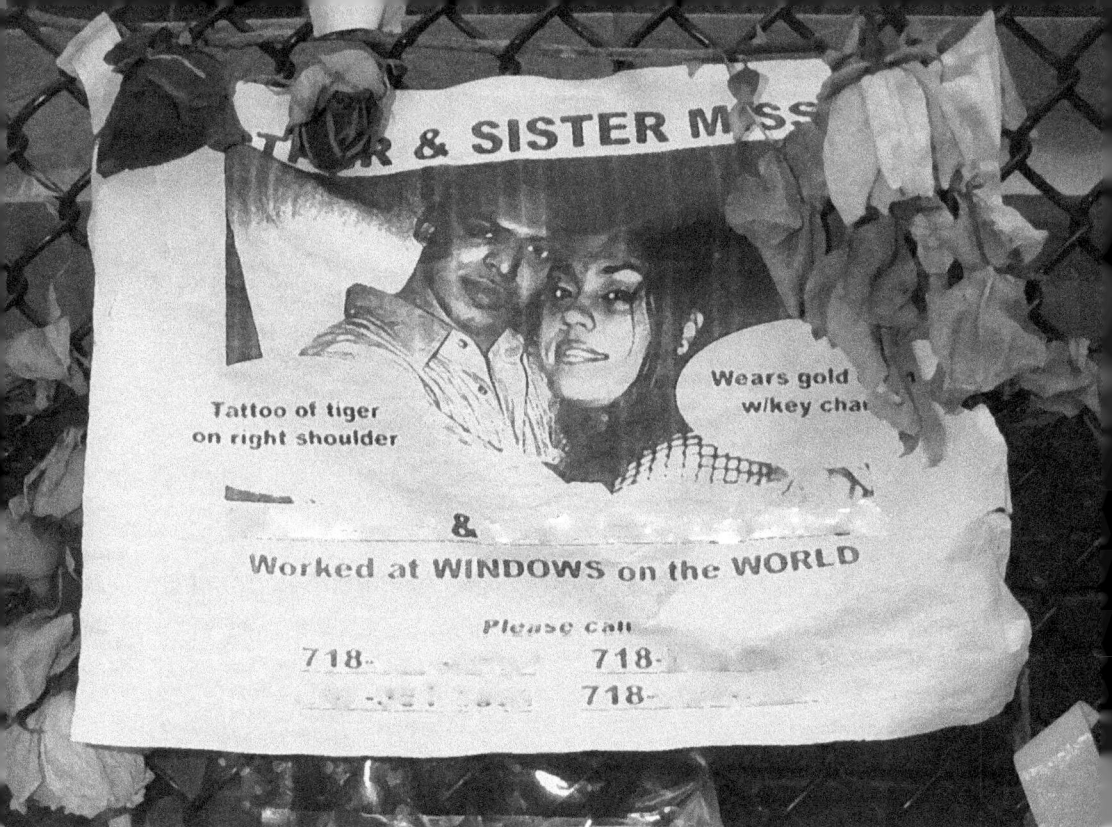

BROTHER & SISTER MISSING

Tattoo of tiger
on right shoulder

Wears gold
w/key cha

&

Worked at WINDOWS on the WORLD

Please call

718-   718-
        -          718-

visages still in their conquering twenties,
snapshot in happy moments,
    embracing their brides,
        babies on knees,
license, yearbook, graduation photos,
smiling at beach or barbecue,
ink fading or bleeding now
    in the sky's abundant tearfall.

In the language we use
for the recovery of wayward pets,
these posters beg the impossible:

<119>

IF ANYONE HAS SEEN HER —
    MISSING — MISSING
LEFT SHOULDER SCAR —
A DOLPHIN TATTOO —
MISSING   —   MISSING
HAVE YOU SEEN ME?—
MISSING — MISSING
PLEASE FIND ME
MISSING — MISSING
WORLD TRADE CENTER

—September 30, 2001, New York City

<120>

ANNIVERSARIUS XXXV

SOMETHING THERE IS IN THE ATTIC

Every human body is a haunted house.
Something there is in the attic
that drives it and sets it course.
Are the shutters half-drawn?
Are they nailed against sunrise?
Do spiders spin in the tenantless rooms?
Who lives there? Ahab and his mono-
Moby madness? Emily with her dry-
leaf poems like money under a bed?
Or no one at all? Does no one hear
as each flaked shingle falls,
as varicose ivy beards up, as sun

<121>

and sag gray-wash the porch beams
and lintels? Something there is
in the attic that drives it and
sets its course. Whose will? An old
man's will? A boy's? A loud-mouthed
betrayer of dreams? A dreamer
paralyzed? Why does this house
not fall, but stand at elmward avenue,
accusing all, begging a moon,
a clean sweep, a neighbor's knock,
a letter? Something there is
in the attic that drives it and
sets its course. This house is
Ahab's ship, Usher's manse, Lovecraft's
infirmary, a witch house, feast
hall, love nest and chapel, sanctum
of Solitude, the Capulets' tomb.

If every human body is a haunted
house, shall we not choose
these ghosts? Can I not summon
a typing poltergeist, a coloratura
howler, a phantom raconteur
to teach me all dead languages,
a gourmet chef insomniac,
someone for whom the 1812 Overture
has not (as for me) ever lost its charm,
a friend who hovers over Batman comics
and knows every line poor Bela Lugosi
was ever made to utter. Room enough,
and beds, and food and tea, for them all!

In October this house is avalanched,
as leaves, and ghosts of leaves
from every tree that ever crisped
in the tug between slant-sun and frost,
pile high in ziggurats of oak,
maple and sumac, hawthorne and willow,

<122>

each with a tale of hope and sorrow
waiting its turn for harvest.
They almost obscure the house, so high
that one lone cupola, the poet's watch,
stands apex at its pyramid,
as one mad vane whirls at the whim
of indecisive winds, as lightning rod
trembles for discharge of the weighted sky
into the attic haunter's cranium.

I am that attic Something: I drive
this house unchanging, wall-to-wall
with mad cargo. My gambrel roof
is an upside-down Mayflower
as I sail against the leaf-tide. Monsters
would block my passage: great whales

of Doubt breach above a maple current;
the baleful skyward eye and tentacles
of the giant squid of Loneliness float by
in a sea-tide of weeping willow.

Yet something there is in the attic
that billows the sails, and drives me on.
The madness that fills these pages
is self-sustaining: some days
these scratchings seem meaningless,
unmusical; some days I read and gasp
and shudder to think that somehow I wrote
or was written through, to reach this apogee.
Alone? Well, lacking the guests
I crave, I must split and become them.
Books, cat and bed, a galaxy of music,
teapot that fills as fast as I empty it:
it is not a bad life,
to be the haunter of one's cobwebbed self.

—Circa 1974, revised July 2, 2011

<123>

ANNIVERSARIUS XXXVI

AUTUMN

Adapted from the a Fragment by Alexander Pushkin, 1833.

"To the drowsy intellect, all things are possible..."
— Derzhavin

I
October! It comes at last. The grove shakes
from naked boughs the last reluctant leaves.
The road is iced with autumn's chilling breath –
I hear the brook behind the turning mill,
but the pond is still; a neighbor with dogs
tramps to the distant fields – his hounds disturb
the peace of forest, his horse's hoof-falls
knock down and trample the winter wheat.

<124>

II
My season now! Spring is a bore to me.
The dull thaw: mud everywhere thick and vile—
Spring dizzies me, as my mind obsesses
daydreaming, my blood in giddy ferment.
Winter's austerity is what I need,
white snows beneath a whiter moon – what joy
to glide airily in a speeding sleigh
with one whose clasping fingers burn like fire!

III
The fun of it, skating steel-shod on ice,
tracing a pattern on the river's face!
The air aglow with winter's festivals!
But even Winter palls – no one can love
six months of snowfall – even the cave bear
in his drowsy den would say "Enough, now!"
Sleigh-rides with jolly youths grow tedious,
and we grow quarrelsome cooped in all day.

IV
You, peach-fuzz Summer – you I could cherish,
except for heat and dust, and biting flies.
These bring dullness. The sated heart wears down.
Our inspiration is a dried-up creek.
Iced tea is not enough; we turn to drink,
we rue the Winter hag, whose funeral
served up wine and blini. What little chill
we get comes from the freezer, sweet and cold.
We spoon out ices, and we think of snow.

<125>

V
No, the end of Autumn is not admired:
But I, reader, will hear no ill of her;
She is the unnoticed child, the wistful
one, way down the line of gaudy sisters.
Her quiet beauty is the one for me.
Her bare-tree starkness, I frankly say
makes Winter's edge the finest time of all.
I love her humbly and so silently
that I alone, in leaf-fall, deserve her.

VI
How can I make you see, Spring-clad lovers?
It is like loving a sickly maiden,
doomed to a consumptive death, pale-skinned
with that ivory pallor and passive gaze,
too weak to hurl a reproach at this life.
Even as her soul expires, her young lips
curl up in a ghost of a febrile smile.
She does not hear her grave being readied.
Today she lives – she is gone tomorrow.

VII
Season of mournful pomp, you live for me!
Your valedictory beauty, mine!
(Or am I yours – tranced and captivated?)
I love to watch as Nature's dyes dim out,
the forest full court in gold and purple,
turned to paler shades in hoarfrost reaping.
The noisy wind tells me its secrets, pale skies
concealed by the billows of darkling clouds,
holding the sun back, frostbite hovering,
whispered threats of grizzled Winter – I hear you!

<126>

VIII

I bloom afresh each time the Autumn comes.
The Russian cold is good for me, I think!
The days' routines regain their old relish.
I sleep and eat in proper proportion.
Desire awakes – and I am young again!
My heart beats fast with rejuvenated
blood – I'm full of life like a newly-fed
Dracula – a lightning-jolted Franken—
well, anyway, you get my meaning, friend!

IX

Bring me my horse! The steppes are calling me!
On his back, glad rider, I'll thump and thud,
fill the dale with my echoing thunder.
His shining hooves strike sparks, his streaming mane
repeats the wind like a Cossack's banner.
The bright ice creaks when we cross the river.
But the days are so short! Already dark!
I read my book in guttering hearth-light,
nourishing immortal longings again.

<127>

X

And in the silence sweet I forget you
(Sad to admit, but everyone and all
seem not to be when I'm lulled by fancy.)
Sit there – empty – wait for the Muse to come –
I am troubled again with lyric fever.
My soul shakes, it reverberates, it wants
to burst the dam of reticence, I dream
of how the verses I've not yet finished
will pour down Time, cross into languages
unknown to me, leap continents and seas,
the children that my visions bore, upright
complete and singing for all to hear them!
Invisible throngs fill me – demon? Muse?
ancestor poets? poets yet to come?—
Take me! Fill my reveries! Make these songs!

XI

So I'll say everything I meant to say.
The brave thoughts have come – rhymes run to meet them
on winged feet. My fingers reach for the pen,
and the neglected pen says "Ink! And where's
that yellow tablet whose narrow green lines
seem always to pull the right words downward?"
Just wait – a little tea – just hold the pen –
wait calmly and the verses will follow.
Thus a still ship slumbers on a still sea.
Hark: chimes! now all hands leap to the rigging.
Exhale! the sails are filled with ideas,
they belly in the wind – the groaning mast –
the monster poem moves to deep water –
the harbor far behind the foaming track.

XII

It sails, but where is this ship taking me?...

<128>

ANNIVERSARIUS XXXVII

THE BLACK HUNTSMAN

(After Victor Hugo's *Le chasseur noir*)

"Who goes there? You, passer-by,
why choose these somber woods,
vast crowds of crows a-flutter —
no place to be with a rainstorm coming!"
"Make way! I am the one
who moves in shadow.
Make way! — for the Black Huntsman!"
The leaves on the trees,
    which the wind has stirred,
are whistling, and I have heard
that all this forest
    will be a-shiver with shrieks
when the storm-cloud clears
and the moon shines down
on the Witches' Sabbath!

Why tarry here? Go chase the doe,
run down the fallow deer,
out of the forest to the unplowed fields.
And more than deer: this is your night
to bag a Tsar, or at least,
an archduke of Austria,
    O Black Huntsman!

<129>

The leaves on the trees —
    Hasten, Black Huntsman,
    to sound your horn-call,
    fasten your leggings
    for a long ride.

The easy stag who comes grazing
    in plain sight by the manor?
    Ah, no, ride down the King,
    ride down a Bishop or two,
        Black Huntsman!

The leaves on the trees —
    It rains, the thunder
    roars, the flood
    sends rivers raging.
    Refuge engulfed, the fox
    flees this way, that way,
    no shelter anywhere, no hope!
    Take not the easy prey:
    there goes a spy on horseback,
    there a judge in his carriage —
        take *them*, Black Huntsman!

The leaves on the trees —
    Do not be moved
    by those monastic flutterings
    in the wild oat-fields,
    those spasms of St. Anthony's
        Satanic possession.
    Hunt down the abbot,
    spare not the monk,
        O Black Huntsman!

<130>

The leaves on the trees—
    Your hounds are on the scent.
    Go for the bears;
    leave no wild boar unslaughtered.
    And while you're at it,
    doing what you do so well,
    Black Huntsman,
    hunt down the Pope, the Emperor!

The leaves on the trees —
    The wily wolves side-step you,
    so loose the pack upon them.
    A stream! The track is lost
    in a teeming waterfall.
But what is this? A president
    without his secret service men!
    And there in that cave,
    a vice-president cowering!
    Run, hounds! Bring them to ground!
        Well done, O Black Huntsman!

The leaves on the trees,
    which the wind has stirred
    are falling, and I have heard
    that the dark Sabbath
    with all its raucous shrieks
    has fled the forest.
    The cloud is pierced
    by the cock's bright crow:
    the dawn is here!

All things regain their original force.
My nation becomes herself again,
    so beautiful to behold,
a white archangel robed in light,
    even to you, Black Huntsman!

<131>

The leaves on the trees,
    which the wind has stirred
    are falling, and I have heard
    that the dark Sabbath
    with all its raucous shrieks
    has fled the forest.
    The cloud is pierced
    by the cock's bright crow:
    the dawn is here!

August 21, 2008
From Victor Hugo's Chatiments: *"Le Chasseur noir"*

<132>

AUTUMN ON PLUTO

Charon has set
　　below the Plutonian horizon.
Beneath the dimmer satellites,
　　desolate Nix and even dimmer Hydra,[1]
an autumn tree of volcanic glass
　　glints like a spiderweb, leaf-cups
athirst for lunar light, weak beams
　　more doubt than promise,

orbs almost black in total blackness,
real only in those eye-blinks
when they occlude some distant star.

Blue-black obsidian limbs
　　cascade to branchlets,
death-willow leaflets serrated and thin,
　　not falling (as there is no wind
　　　　here ever) but *flung*
with crossbow efficiency,
　　a flight of tri-lobed arrows
sharper than surgical knives.

The only red of this world's autumn
　　is blood-flow as deer
(the stock and store of Hades)
　　collapse in agony,
and silicon roots thrust funnel
　　and thirsty filament
to drink from the spreading rust
of severed carotids,

---

[1] Nix and Hydra were discovered by the Hubble Telescope in 2005.

<133>

pierced hearts pumping,
antler and bone and hide
a-pile the slaughter-field.

After a few weeks' wintering,
    the branchlets crackle and split
as red-berry buds form perfect spheres,
Pluto's cornelian cherries,[2]
untouched, inedible
amid the bone and gemstone clutter
    of dead Arcady.

Not far from Acheron's turgid flow
(nitrous ice in a methane river),
dread Hades dreams of venison,
afloat in sauce of cornelian cherry.
Persephone wipes clean
    his fevered brow, proffers
a bowl of wheat-porridge
    and raisins, the flesh
of olive and apricot. He sighs.
She can only make
    what her mother Ceres taught her.

---

[2] Although consecrated to Apollo, the fruit of the cornelian cherry tree was
believed to be the food of the dead in Hades.

<134>

The juice of venison has never
    run down her chin, nor has
she savored the sourest of cherries
drowned in bee-honey.

He must count the days
    till her vernal journey upward,
till he can pluck the victims
from beneath the kill-deer willow,
fill baskets with precious cornel fruit,

then call forth poets and heroes,
    (Hephaestus and Mars as well
    if he's in a generous spirit)
for a bone-gnaw feast
around the lava pit,
a bard- and-boast orgy
of odes and war-talk.

It goes on for weeks, and
although the words they speak
are apt to freeze between one's mouth
and the receiving ear,
for the summer-widower Hades,
death is a bowl of cherries.

<135>

ANNIVERSARIUS XXXIX

NIGHTS AT THE STRAND

The Strand Theater, Scottdale, PA

As the lights dim and the tattered curtain
rustled and parted with a creak-crank
of unseen wheels and pulleys, as a boy's eyes
widen to a dark screen grown suddenly bright
and huge – not the tiny ovoid TV
but vast, enormous, spanning the width
of his field of vision from Row Three,
the row, as Marilyn tells him
with a fifth-grader's knowing accent
the monsters are in perfect focus.

<136>

He cleans his glasses furiously
as the sound track crackles, and a globe
topped with the RKO tower emanates
a zig-zag of Marconi waves, and, lo,
he commences his movie-watching Saturdays
with *King Kong*, who, on that screen,
amid those shrieks and screams of the crowd
on-screen and in the audience, strides tall
on his island, taller yet as he scales
the uncountable floors of the Empire State.
He had seen cartoon dinosaurs, but those
who try to wrest the Fay Wray-morsel from Kong
are as real as they get, the first taste
of a primal world of eat-and-be-eaten,
smite-or-be-smitten, the first beware
of the fate of him who falls for Beauty.

An old poet now, on a far coast, he can, if asked,
recite all the names of the movies he saw there
like a litany, week by week, in double-feature pairs,
as dear to him as the saint days to a medieval monk.

A basement full of surgical failures in *The Black Sleep* –
first view of an exposed brain a special thrill.
They do that to crazy people in Torrance, he's told,
skull-top raised up like an egg-cup, brains
poked and stirred around for no more reason
than *Let's see what happens if we do this.*
The mute sad butler played by Lugosi was a pathetic sight;
the man who had been Dracula reduced to a doorman.
Rathbone and Carradine, Tamirov and Johnson
the mad doctor and his henchmen and victims.
This double-billed with *The Creeping Unknown,*
whose alien-microbed astronaut, gaunt and wandering,
assimilates all life in its path: men, cacti and lions,

<137>

until it oozes octopoid onto the scaffolding
around Westminster Abbey. Fast work
for stalwart scientist Quatermass who rigs
the metalwork with a million volts
from a nearby power plant.

After *The Blob* he turned inward to his chemistry set
and devised, with his friends, The Boron Monster, z
      a bubbling mess
of boric acid, carbonates, and a medley of insect parts
that festered for two days in a Florence flask, then
made a nocturnal exeunt into the floor drain. For weeks
the four boys of the Kingview Science Club swore they
          heard it
in house pipes and gurgling drains; one went so far
as to say it raised its white pseudopods when he looked
into the late-night toilet bowl.
                    The dreaded Cyclops
from *The Seventh Voyage of Sinbad* seemed as he woke
to stand in silhouette against the bare hill behind his house.
When the garish colors of *Curse of Frankenstein*
reveled in blood and bosoms, he set up shop
in Caruso's garage in Keiffertown. *Live Monster Show*,
the hand-drawn poster said in drip-red lettering
and the children came from all around.
Clothesline and sheet for curtain, old 78
of *The Sheik of Araby* a Gothic foxtrot,
his fellow fourth-graders no longer chemists
but grease-paint actors: monster and villagers,
doctor and hunchback. Naturally *he* is the Doctor,
his hands the ones that raise Jell-O brains and send blood
rivulets down the aisles among the screaming girls.
A raincoat, sleeves inverted, can pass for a Dracula cape.
He sends for a mail order course in hypnotism.
They learn the art of mummy-wrapping (green chalk
and Noxema), black powder and kerosene for fires,
dry ice for malevolent Jekyll-Hyde elixirs.

<138>

But there's no keeping up with the Strand and its
accelerating horrors. The bugs have invaded:
ant and tarantula, mantis and locust grown
to the size of locomotives, the dark side
of the atom whose giant flower mutations
they are taught about on schooldays. They would
all glow in the dark and in perfect health
when Our Friend the Atom was done with them.
After *Them!* and *Tarantula, Beginning of the End,*
The Giant Claw, and *The Deadly Mantis,*
the worst was *The Black Scorpion,* so horrible,
in fact, that as he watched it open a train
like a sardine can, extract the passengers, then sting
them with its terrible stinger before the slow
ascent to the drooling jaws and mandibles, someone
on the balcony vomited a visual melange
of popcorn and orange soda on his brother's shoulders.

Then came Godzilla, a whole new order
of urban destruction and radium-breath:
boys who had never seen a city looked on
as powerlines and factories, gas terminals and seaports,
glass and steel towers, department stores and palaces
were stamped to splinters and rubble
beneath the wayward reptilian scourge
that had nothing to do with eating: Godzilla was hell-rage,
a force that might wipe clean the earth once and forever
of the human infestation.
                              Godzilla made manifest, too,
in the form of a fat bully on Mulberry Street
who waited to knock the school and library books
from his hands into the nearest snowdrift.
He filled a squirt gun with ammonia and onion juice,
a minor armament since he was studying nuclear fission
and knew a dozen withering curses in Latin.

<139>

When the saucers of *The Mysterians* began airlifting women
to help repopulate a dying world, he was jealous,
dreamt of a gravity beam abduction from his own bed,
to an orphan life among interesting creatures.
Forbidden Planet taught him to embrace the alien:
if left on Altair Four he would happily join Morbius
in solitary study of the long extinct Krell geniuses;
if taxed enough with unjust bullying, he would join
the crew of Nemo's Nautilus: they'd all be sorry
when he sank half the Atlantic fleet or turned
the submarine to starship and beat the Russians to Mars.
He had never been two towns away,
    but he knew the names of the outer planets' moons.

Small boy in torn shoes and baggy hand-me-downs
sewn from his father's old shirts,
goggle-eyed with wrong glasses, arms full
of comics and all the books he could carry,
he was The Strand's acolyte, its screen and stage
the doorway to a higher reality. No matter
how far he has gone, what written or done,
he is still there, in that seat in Row Three
as the ships land, the invasion commences,
the tentacle comes slowly into focus
at the edge of vision, the branches part
to those two great orbs of The Beast.

He was the one who ran away
    to join the Monsters
        to explore the stars,
haunted, to become the Haunter.

*October 2010 – March 2011, after a visit to the
Geyer Performing Arts Center, Scottdale, PA,
in the restored Strand Theater Building.*

<140>

BAI HU, THE WHITE TIGER

1
I dreamt — it was no dream! —
for there, on the floor, the melted snow,
the window-lattice broken, night coals
from the brazier scattered everywhere.
I dreamt he was there beside me:

the great white cat, tiger of Siberia,
lord of Manchurian wastelands. He,
my servant comes trembling to tell me,
has taken up residence
at the far end of the north pavilion.

"Ah! let him stay! Bring me my sword‽
No! my pen and scroll! I must wash
my thoughts with a draught of tea.
Renew the fire. Refill the *yi xing*
pot with pale white tea leaves."

"He is Death," my servant tells me.
"Bai Hu, the White Tiger,
has roamed these hills for half
a thousand years. He has no mate;
They say he is Hunger incarnate.
With fire and gong and beaten shields
we can drive him away forever."

I shake my head and answer:
"Bai Hu is welcome here, Old Chen.
He is Autumn, the world's Fall,
my autumn, the end of my youth.

<142>

Where he treads, frost follows,
his breath the snow that fells the wheat
and makes the maples scream
red murder. Long have I known
he would be my guest one day."

"Cover the window," old Chen admonishes.
He shudders as a chill breeze enters
and the willows begin shivering.
"I will send for torchmen to light your way,
an escort of our bravest youths."

Already I see two feline eyes alight.
They grow larger in the passageway.
"It is too late. A guest once past the threshold
must be offered food and lodging.
The tiger may come and go as he pleases."

<143>

I point to where the great beast enters.
My servant issues a piercing cry.
Ignoring us, the monster, white
in the whiter moonlight, lies down
on the warm tiles of the coal hearth.

I return to my calligraphy.
"You see, Old Chen, how he reclines.
I do not think he means to harm me."
Chen bows and backs to the doorway,
and as he closes the double door, calls back,
"Bai Hu no longer hunts by night, but
tomorrow brings terror to the countryside.

The tiger will kill the fallow deer,
and, should you venture forth by daylight,
he, pretending not to know you,
will turn on you as well. Your kindness
will all too soon be forgotten. An old poet
is sweet fruit after a venison banquet."

<144>

2
Oh night of nights for Tiger and Poet!
'Twixt Venus and Jupiter, one moon
hangs crescent; 'twixt sleep and dawn
the great beast cradles me, and I, him;
sword, fang, and claw forgotten, defying
our double death; a frozen interval,
two hearts abeat, and four lungs breathing.
I dream of being a great beast, rampant;
the tiger dreams of the calligraphy brush,
the tail-flick ink flow that places songs
on paper, words in the ears
of unborn readers and listeners.
I taste the blood in his mouth, the flex
of great legs that can overleap all prey;
he tastes pale tea and delicate sauces,
the savor of rare wine in a heated bowl.

3
My guest is gone when I awaken.
As dawn breaks through,
the Heaven-tree, the willow boughs,
the distant pines sigh, shiver, shrug:
they will fight for a green day,
bird-harboring, leaf-tipped
to the lambent sunbeams.
Somewhere, out there, the tiger
drags Fall behind him as he hunts
life down with a panther frenzy.
Great clouds of birds assemble and flee
before him; cave, den, and warren
pull in their denizens for the long sleep
of winter. He leaves a trail
of antlered skeletons, doe-widows,
trees clawed clean of summer.

<146>

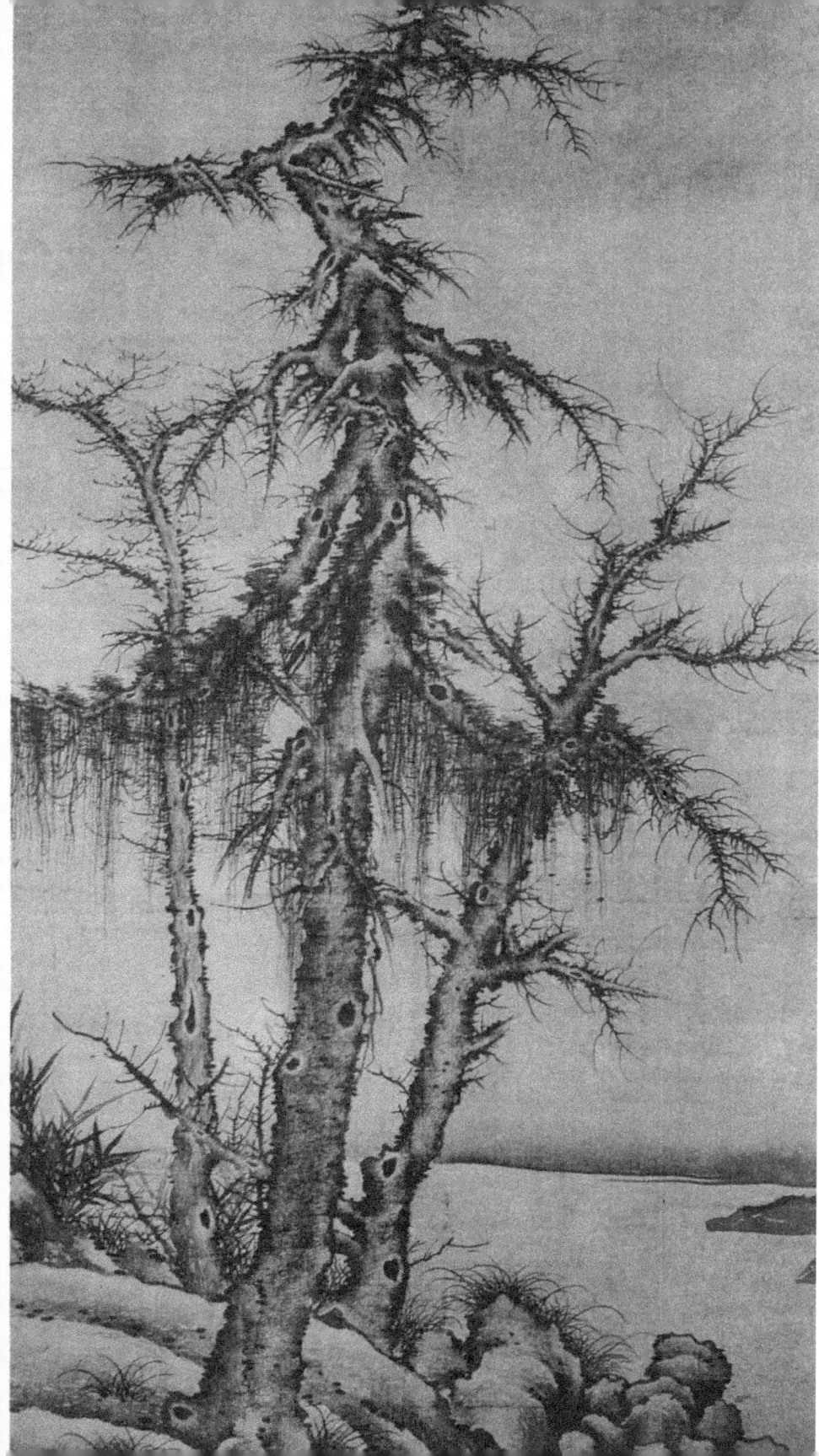

4

My place is here with lamp and teapot.
I write a poem. I roll and seal
the rice-paper scroll, wipe clean
the brush and close the ink-jar.
This is not just any autumn's beast.
There is some cause for which
he spares me; he is not *my* Autumn
nor the death-breath of *my* last winter.
I have ink enough for a thousand more poems.

No, Bai Hu is the Tiger of Entropy:
he drags tornados, kill-winds
and glaciers behind him.
He would blink out
the world's great cities if he could;
he would strike down the moon
as his ball-of-string plaything,
leave earth an orphan
in a sunless cosmos.

If I let him.

Tomorrow, while *he* sleeps,
wherever he sleeps —
    and I see the place,
    in the shade of the pines
    beyond the placid river —
I shall send Chen for my finest mount,
my armor and my banner men.
I shall ride forth,
my flag the Three-No poem of summer
defiance: *No* to death,
No to surrender, *No* to the idea
that all things must have their autumn.

<148>

5

At the second dawn, we set forth
            on our fastest ponies.
I have sixty-one years
as I leave the pavilion.
I have fifty-one years as I cross
the great wheat fields.
I have forty-one years
as I track the maple-red forest.
I have thirty-one years
as I ford the river,
horse-neck and saddle
just barely above the water.
I have twenty-one years
as Old Chen passes to me
the great halberd
of my ancestors.

Now, I shall kill the White Tiger

— 2010, rev. 2011

<150>

ABOUT THE POEMS

The poems in *Anniversarius* span 43 years of life and writing. I began in 1968, when I was an impoverished college student gloomy about the political prospects for mankind, and brought this poem cycle to its close — or so I thought — in 1996, when a wave of major revisions brought the first 27 poems to a close. In between, the melancholic college student moved to New York and had an active career as printer, small press publisher, writer and consultant. Then he pulled up roots in 1985 and moved to New England, living in Providence and Boston, returning to New York in 1994, then back to Providence for good a few years later. Thus there are three distinct landscapes in which autumns are marked and commemorated — a sleepy, Pennsylvania village with its lakeside pioneer graveyard; the great megalopolis of Manhattan; and the haunted gambrel-roofed towns of New England.

When I published the third expansion of this cycle in 1996, I believed that I was finished with this project: I expected to write more "autumnals," of course, but I expected to treat them as unconnected works, to be gathered in other collections. In mid-2011, I commenced a major revision and editing process on all my poetic works, and I came to realize that there were now 40 poems that belonged together in a longer, almost symphonic cycle. I let the original edition stand as "Ring 1," and the newer poems became "Ring 2." I regard this cycle as a single, integrated work, not only as variations on the theme of autumn, but also as a survey of all my varied moods, interests, and experiences. Events of import in the intervening years, including 9/11 and the U.S. war in Iraq; my departure from New York once again for Providence; the new life I commenced in academia starting in 2003; and my return to my childhood haunts in Pennsylvania (some not seen since I was thirteen), all figure in Ring 2, which ends, to no one's surprise more than mine, in Ming-era China with a tiger hunt.

Across this landscape of poems I have chased my own literary heroes. I stood with Poe on Morton Street Pier, waxed Shelleyan in Madison Square Park, and then tread in Poe's and H.P. Lovecraft's steps in Providence, Salem, Marblehead and Boston. Through these poems, I have also traced my own philosophy and metaphysics. I invent and play with monsters, mock and defeat gods, soar transcendentally among the planets, lament the death of innocents and friends, and declare my strange and solitary psyche.

A few words about style. My poetry is neo-Romantic, yet post-Whitman. Although free in form, it is unabashedly uninfluenced by modernism. Until very recently, I wrote no rhymed poems. In revising the oldest poems, I felt tempted, while making imagery and meaning more lucid, to make

<151>

the language more beautiful by employing more formal methods. It's an experiment that gives me pleasure. A young listener surprised me recently by asking whether my long-lined poems were influenced by Ginsberg. I had to say "Yes," because I learned the improvisational long-breathed line from Whitman and Ginsberg, even if I have turned out to be more lyrical, old-fashioned poet at the end. I can and do write in form, but I prefer the sudden inspiration that lets lines flow onto the page with a continual play of rhythm, consonance and alliteration. I serve not Apollo, but Hermes, the god of sudden inspiration and the bringer of dreams. Revision can hone away imperfections and make lines more regular, but I prefer the impulse that reworks and expands upon an older poem, making it anew with new knowledge and the perspective of longer life. Revision for me often entails more expanding than expunging.

If asked whose poems and whose world-views found their ways into these poems, I would choose a strange mix: Homer, Lucretius and Horace; Shakespeare, Shelley, Hugo and Poe among the Romantics; Whitman, Rilke, Lovecraft and Jeffers for their cosmic consciousness. For style: Whitman, Ginsberg, comic books, Ray Bradbury's stories, and a life of immersion in classical music, the ocean I swim in. I have been aptly called a poet for whom Modernism did not happen. I still believe in muse-possessed voice, the Poet, and the Reader. A thousand coincidences in the writing of these poems mark me as one who trusts in a universe wired for poetry and brimming with meaning.

Pleasure is the optimal word here. I intend these poems to be objects made of beautiful language, containing vivid images and provocative ideas. A few are fleeting moods that I do not necessarily agree with, such as the cynical "Green Things Are Melancholy," while others are my attempts to define the immutable nature of things. Some are meant to be read and to be *read aloud* as rhapsodies to and of the Autumn. Since other poems are narrative, political, or satirical, these use autumn as a stage for other purposes.

I do not think of *Anniversarius* as a gloomy book, despite all the imagery associated with autumn. I am proud of the cycle and happy with its arc of ideas and the culmination of each of the two "Rings."

<152>

The following notes summarize what I might say to explain the poems before reading them to an audience.

BETWEEN THE PAGES, and its Spanish version ENTRE LAS HOJAS, is a lyrical poem that serves as an overture, on a Rossini scale, to the work that follows. I wrote the Spanish version (a new poem rather than a word-for-word translation) to begin what I hope will be a process of writing for the hemisphere. We owe our amazing Latin American poets the compliment of writing back to them in their own beautiful language.

AUTUMN ELEGY has been rewritten several times. I was a student at Edinboro State College (now Edinboro University of Pennsylvania) in 1968, and this poem came to me on the morning of the first snow of the year. Its sudden turn to the elegiac surprised me — I was thinking, without quite knowing it, of my fellow students being drafted and sent off to the senseless war in Vietnam.

THE LINDEN TREE IN PRAGUE, originally titled "In Prague, A Tree of Many Colors," was my reaction to the Soviet-led invasion of Czechoslovakia in 1969. The student Jan Palach became an icon of rebellion by setting himself afire to protest the invasion of his country. I held back this poem for many years, unhappy with some of its language. By 1996, I thought the poem was finished and I included it here and in my collection, *Twilight of the Dictators*. By 2011, details suppressed for many years by the Communist regime in Czechoslovakia, were available, and I was able to extend the narrative into the events of 1989. It came to me in an instant that the undefined tree of the old poem should be a linden tree, so I added details characteristic of that tree (a familiar one from the streets of Providence). After identifying the tree I discovered that the linden tree is an emblem of the Czech Republic. After all these years, I think the poem tells the whole story, and the tree-as-narrator has been clarified.

THE ISLAND existed only as a random journal note; it makes an effective bridge to carry me from Edinboro to New York.

AUTUMN SONGS are lyrics of love found and lost. The second is inspired by the poetry of John Donne, and is an aria in the sense that it can, and should, be read in a single long breath.

<153>

WITH POE ON MORTON STREET PIER was rewritten many times over the years. The early drafts were cityscape impressions only. Poe was added years later when I discovered that he had first disembarked in Manhattan on this spot.

THE PUMPKINED HEART reflects how much I hated New York City in the early days of my stay, and how I yearned for the beautiful landscape of Pennsylvania. This became the title poem of my second chapbook and was for many years my "homesick" poem.

LET WINTER COME is ironic. It's a poem about not wanting to write another poem, and about feeling old and finished, at age twenty-five!

I PERSIST IN GREEN is about a stubborn tree that refuses to change with the seasons. I always knew there was more to this poem than met the eye, and successive revisions have finally brought out its full depth.

OCTOBER RECKONINGS is a curiosity, but one I am less happy about. An opening verse, written freely, is then "mirrored" by working some of the images, rhythms and words backwards.

THE GRIM REAPER names the unnamable and speaks face to face to Death — easy to do when you know that "my time is not yet come."

DEAD LEAVES THE EMBLEMS TRUEST was written in Madison Square Park in New York. It is my answer to Shelley and Whitman, and my clarion for a natural world that is transcendental without a god in it. The defiant Shelley of *Prometheus Unbound* has always been close to my soul.

GREEN THINGS ARE MELANCHOLY has gotten me in lots of trouble. It is dour and cynical. I didn't agree with it even as the ink was drying, but the poem has a life of its own. I can't suppress this ugly baby — instead, I recast it in formal rhyme and added even more melancholia to make it all it can be. Pass it by if you can't take it.

AUTUMN PORTENTS is a bagatelle, a reflection of the political landscape of the year.

TWO FULL MOONS IN OCTOBER reacts to a simple fact of the calendar: now and then, a 31-day month gets two full moons. The photograph is a Margritte take on the title.

THE ORIONID METEORS was my happy discovery that October hosts a major meteor shower.

OCTOBER IS COMING! brings a large scale back to the cycle. It marks my departure from New York in 1985 and the beginning of my New England adventure. It is Whitmanesque, daring, joyful. It launched the most productive three years of my writing life.

THE STATE VERSUS AUTUMN is a libertarian protest against book banners and would-be book burners. I don't recall the specific events that triggered it, but I recall returning to Edinboro for a symposium and being astonished at hearing some of the radical professors from the 1960s now

<154>

advocating banning *Huckleberry Finn* for high school students. There were also a few hoax-scares about teen-age Satanic cults going on around that time, and I almost certainly saw some editorials protesting Halloween as a detestable pagan holiday.

SON OF DRACULA was originally just a short poem, with a recollection of strange autumn images seen from a hospital room when I was fifteen. I have hugely expanded this poem and made it more explicitly autobiographical. It is the only poem in Ring 1 that treats of what passed before in my life. The "hated town" in which is takes place is not Scottdale, the town of my birth which I rediscovered in 2011, but West Newton, where I was forced to live after my parents were divorced. (More grisly details of this will be in the new edition of *The Pumpkined Heart*.)

NOT YEARS ENOUGH is easy to understand for those who saw my library, with books filling whole walls and spilling over into hallways. I gave away or sold some 4,000 books in recent years, and I still won't live long enough to read those that remain. But who said that a bibliophile has to read all the things he buys?

THE SAILOR AND THE OAK NYMPHS is a narrative poem including the three oak tree nymphs from Greek mythology. It's not really necessary to know any mythology to enjoy it.

END OF THE WORLD is a narrative based on a whimsy. As I was speeding through New England on a train, I wondered what it would be like if the trees kept their leaves and the people turned colors and blew away instead. I think it was also influenced by seeing a hysterical Evangelical comic book depicting The Rapture.

THE OUTSIDER is the closest thing I have done to a poetic self-portrait. If you want to know who I am, this poem says it all.

FRAGMENTS OF A HYMN TO RHEA, THE OAK TREE GODDESS, is a very specialized poem, containing just about everything that's known about the Chthonic figure of Rhea. I cast the poem in imitation of Middle English verse, with alliteration and caesura, in an attempt to convey, in English, a sense of the antiquity of the ideas and characters. This is very specialized stuff, but I

<155>

include it because it connects autumn imagery with the very root of Western mythology.

RUNAWAYS is a simple poem, a re-expression of how important trees are to us. I have seen people in New England get more upset over the destruction of a tree than over a murder. We need to reflect on why we surround ourselves with trees and what they mean to us. The goddess Rhea, or a Druid priest, lurks closer to the surface of the psyche than we know.

IN CHILL NOVEMBER is a late autumn poem, written during a train ride. I reflected that since everything looked equally dead in the landscape, there was no way to tell the difference between a dead tree and once which had merely shed its leaves.

Returning to Edinboro after more than a decade of absence, I was shocked to see a chain-link fence built around my favorite graveyard. My anger is vented in THE FENCE. I am pleased to hear that some art students took up my challenge and cut some holes in the fence.

TO THE ARC OF THE SUBLIME was written after a late night sojourn in some woods near the Seekonk River in Providence. This was truly a visionary night, and I knew right away that the *Anniversarius* cycle had reached its apex. This poem ends "Ring 1."

The second part of the cycle begins with CREEPERS, an earlier poem that began as New York City impressions from a Halloween night, and then grew into something a little more. It is an impressionistic piece still, a kind of Charles Ives Halloween in Manhattan, with a sinister glance at clinging ivy.

OCTOBER THOUGHTS IN WAR-TIME takes place on a moonlit night on Providence's Benefit Street and takes its mood from the anxious thought of living, once again in "war-time," this one longer in duration than all of World War II.

I wrote LOVED ONES when my friend and former professor Don Washburn chided me, in his role as a Sufi master, for not "pursuing the Beloved."

AUTUMN ON MARS is for Ray Bradbury, a tribute to the author of *The Martian Chronicles*.

ON RECEIVING A GIFT OF BOOKS IN EARLY OCTOBER was a writing experiment: hurling the contents of a carton of books on the floor and reading around at random.

AUTUMN SUNDAYS IN MADISON SQUARE PARK is based on journal notes describing Madison Square Park across more than a decade. Those enjoying this beautiful, restored park today will have little idea how rundown and decrepit it had become. It took a long time to cast all these impressions into one poem, with a novel metric scheme.

<156>

SEPTEMBER IN GOTHAM was written September 30, 2001, my first visit to Manhattan after the events of 9/11. I was limited to a tour of midtown and parts of Greenwich Village, and the tattered remnants of the posters describing the missing and dead were tearing off walls and blowing through the streets.

SOMETHING THERE IS IN THE ATTIC was actually drafted in 1974, but never published in any of my books. This 2011 revision places it in the cycle where I think it has always belonged.

AUTUMN is a splendid poem – an unfinished work – by Alexander Pushkin. Somehow I had never paid any special mind to the poem, perhaps because Victorian translations were so stodgy. Pushkin's autumn thoughts are so much in my "manner," that I could not resist making my own new paraphrase of the poem.

THE BLACK HUNTSMAN is an adaptation of Victor Hugo's classic poem, "Le Chasseur Noir." I could not resist incorporating then-President Bush and the war criminal Dick Cheney among the victims of the Huntsman. So many Hugo treasures await discovery and translation.

AUTUMN ON PLUTO was a passing inspiration, a vision of a tree with razor-sharp obsidian leaves. The remainder of the poem flowed from that opening image. Cornelian cheery trees are planted around the Brown University campus, and I enjoy picking and eating "the food of the dead" from their branches.

NIGHTS AT THE STRAND celebrates my happy return, in October 2011, to Scottdale, Pennsylvania, the town of my birth. The movie theater where I saw all those monster movies that so warped my consciousness, had been boarded up in the 1970s, and then purchased and restored lovingly as the Geyer Performing Arts Center. The poem intersperses recollections of the films I saw there starting in the third grade, with actual memories of life in the town. The visit was a profound one for me, restoring a landscape that had been ripped from me.

BAI HU, THE WHITE TIGER, has been rewritten three times in the last two years. I had no inkling of its defiant ending in the earlier versions. The White Tiger, in Chinese painting, is a symbol of autumn. The scholar in his pavilion may be "Meng Ch'iu Lei," a mysterious Ming Dynasty gentleman bearing my Chinese poetry name, which translates as "Dream of Autumn Thunder." It is a suitable coda for my 40-poem symphony of autumn.

<157>

ABOUT THE ILLUSTRATIONS

All illustrations are digital photos or digital art by Brett Rutherford except where noted. These illustrations are in full color in the ebook version of this book, in grayscale in the print edition.

Page 2: Sprague Monument in Swan Point Cemetery, Providence, RI.

Page 10: Portrait of Jan Palach (1969), public domain, Internet.

Page 15: Sassafras leaves on River Road, Providence, RI.

Page 17: Manhattan skyline.

Page 23: Salem (MA) trees in silhouette.

Page 27: Treescape in Scottdale PA.

Page 32: Maple Leaf Carpet, Providence RI.

Page 36: Cornstalks in Scottdale PA park gazebo.

Page 37: Full moon(s) in Providence RI (sepiatone).

Page 44: Dome and Unitarian Church at dusk, Providence, RI.

Page 57: Chinese fan painting, from the digital archive, *Ancient Chinese Painting Masterpieces*.

Page 61: Montage of oak roots and Arthur Rackham's Tree Nymph.

Page 69: Chinese painting from *Ancient Chinese Painting Masterpieces*.

Page 73: Tree roots, Blackstone Park, Providence, RI.

Page 78: City trees in lower Manhattan.

Page 80: Elder maple in Edinboro (PA) pioneer graveyard.

Page 85: Under the maples in Edinboro graveyard.

Page 87: Gravestones at Edinboro.

Page 91: Pond in Blackstone Park, Providence.

Page 95: Ivy on wall, Manhattan.

Page 105: Painting from *Ancient Chinese Painting Masterpieces*.

Page 109: Madison Square Park, New York City.

Page 111: View of Flatiron Building from Madison Square Park.

Pages 113: Word War I Memorial, Madison Square Park (detail).

Pages 115, 117, 118, Missing persons posters from New York City, September 2001.

Page 120: House and tree at Marblehead, MA.

Page 123: Colonial window, rural Rhode Island.

Page 133. Greek pottery painting of Pluto and Persephone (Internet).

Pages 140, 142, 144, 146, 148. Chinese paintings from *Ancient Chinese Painting Masterpieces*.

Page 153: Students protesting Russian invasion of Czechoslovakia.

Page 155: Rhea riding a lion. Original in Museum of Fine Arts, Boston.

<158>

ABOUT THE POET

Brett Rutherford, born in Scottdale, Pennsylvania, began writing poetry seriously during a stay in San Francisco. During his college years at Edinboro State University in Pennsylvania, he published an underground newspaper and printed his first hand-made poetry chapbook. He moved to New York City, where he founded The Poet's Press in 1971. For more than 20 years, he worked as an editor, journalist, printer, and consultant to publishers and nonprofit organizations.

After a literary pilgrimage to Providence, Rhode Island, on the track of H.P. Lovecraft and Edgar Allan Poe, he moved there with his press. *Poems From Providence* was the fruit of his first three years in the city (1985-1988), published in 1991. Since then, he has written a study of Edgar Allan Poe and Providence poet Sarah Helen Whitman (briefly Poe's fiancee), a biographical play about Lovecraft, and his second novel, *The Lost Children* (Zebra Books, 1988). His poetry, in volumes both thematic and chronological, can be found in *Poems From Providence* (1991, 2011), *Things Seen in Graveyards* (2007), *Twilight of the Dictators* (1992, 2009), *The Gods As They Are, On their Planets* (2005), *Whippoorwill Road: The Supernatural Poems* (1998, 2005), and *An Expectation of Presences* (2011).

Returning to school for a master's degree in English, Rutherford completed this project in 2007, and now works for University of Rhode Island in distance learning, and teaches for the Women's Studies Department. There, he has created courses on "The Diva," "Women in Science Fiction," and "Radical American Women." He has prepared annotated editions of Matthew Gregory Lewis's *Tales of Wonder*, the poetry of Charles Hamilton Sorley, A.T. Fitzroy's antiwar novel *Despised and Rejected*, and the first volume of the collected writings of Emilie Glen.

His interests include classical music and opera, and Latin American music; Chinese art, history and literature; bicycling, graveyards, woods, horror films, intellectual history, and crimes against nature.

<159>

ABOUT THIS BOOK

The body text of this book is Schneidler, also known as Stempel Schneidler, designed by F. H. Ernst Schneidler in 1936 for the Bauer Foundry. This was a distinctive hot metal typeface, with cupped serifs, handsome italics and a quirky question mark. The design is inspired by Renaissance Venetian typefaces. The same face was used for the 1996 edition of *Anniversarius*.

The footnotes and prose sections of this book are set in Aldine type, a face inspired by the designs of the great Venetian humanist printer and publisher Aldus Manutius. This type was chosen for its higher legibility in smaller sizes.

Headlines are set in Futura, a Bauhaus-influenced type that came to be one of the most popular sans serif faces of the 20th century. Its geometric emphasis and even width of stroke takes its form from classic Greek column lettering, but looks completely modern because of its strict use of geometric forms (circle and isosceles triangles). The hot metal face was designed in 1927 for the Bauer foundry in Germany.

This book is issued in Adobe Acrobat format with illustrations in full color, and in print with illustrations in grayscale.

<160>